Waves—Not Spoons

101 Strategies for Managing Our Physical, Emotional, and Social Energy

By Gerald Hughes

Waves—Not Spoons

101 Strategies for Managing Our Physical, Emotional, and Social Energy

By Gerald Hughes

Copyright © 2019 Gerald Hughes. All Rights Reserved.

V1.2

The opinions expressed in this manuscript are solely the opinions of the author and do not represent the opinions or thoughts of the publisher. The author has represented and warranted full ownership and/or legal right to publish all the materials in this book.

This book may not be reproduced, transmitted, or stored in whole or in part by any means, including graphic, electronic, or mechanical without the express written consent of the publisher except in the case of brief quotations embodied in critical articles and reviews.

Waves—Not Spoons: 101 Strategies for Managing Our Physical, Emotional, and Social Energy is not intended to replace sound medical advice. Always consult a health professional regarding any physical, mental or emotional issues. This book was written for entertainment purposes and the reader agrees to indemnify and hold harmless the authors and our agents against any use of the information contained herein.

ISBN: 9781679120534

Photos by Unknown Author, licensed under CC BY-SA.

https://creativecommons.org/licenses/by-sa/3.0/legalcode

All rights reserved.

PRINTED IN THE UNITED STATES OF AMERICA

Table of Contents

Preface	5
Introduction	7
Chapter 1: Understanding Waves	9
Chapter 2: Understanding Ourselves	11
• Dominant Brain Functions	11
• Flow of Sensory Information	12
• Dominant Feeling	14
• Dominant Access	16
• Dominant Consideration	17
• Dominant Excitement	18
• Dominant—NOT Exclusive	19
Chapter 3: Personal Waves	20
• Rhythm Waves	20
• Routine Waves	21
• Chronic Illness	22
• Chronic Pain	23
• Wholistic Approach	23
Chapter 4: Physical Energy Waves	24
Chapter 5: Emotional Energy Waves	26
• The Autonomic Nervous System	27
Chapter 6: Social Energy Waves	29

Chapter 7: Relationship Waves   32

- **Masking**   34
- **Impostor Syndrome**   35
- **People Pleasers**   35
- **Abusive Relationships**   36

Chapter 8: Communication Waves   38

- **Communication Styles**   39
- **Visual Communication**   41
- **Visual Listening**   41
- **Visual Speaking**   42
- **Greetings**   43
- **Goodbyes**   44
- **Smalltalk and Chit-Chat**   45
- **Empathy and Rapport**   46

Chapter 9: Family Waves   49

Chapter 10: Waves in the Classroom   51

- **Stress is the Enemy**   52
- **Visual Learning State**   53
- **Visual Reading/Listening**   54
- **Seeing by Touch**   54
- **Patterns and Context**   54
- **Morning Routine**   55
- **Afterschool/Homework Routine**   56
- **Bedtime Routine**   57

Chapter 11: Waves on the Job   58

Chapter 12: Group Event Waves   63

Chapter 13: Public Speaking Waves	65
Chapter 14: Project Management Waves	67
Top-down Project Breakdown	68
Flow-Chart/Mind-Map	69
• Procrastination	70
• Demand Avoidance	70
Chapter 15: Goal Setting	72
• SMART Goal Visualization	73
Chapter 16: Physical Energy Exercises	74
• Breathing Energy Refresh	75
• Get the Blood Flowing	75
• Water, Water, Everywhere	75
• Eat Healthy and Often	76
• Physical Exercise	77
• Guided Imagery	78
• Massage	78
• Acupuncture	78
• Biofeedback	79
Chapter 17: Emotional Energy Refresh	80
• Expanded Awareness; Relax and Focus	81
• Power Nap	81
• Quick Disconnect	81
• Juggling to Relax and Focus	82
• Thumb Juggling	84
• Relax and Focus App	84

- Eye of the Storm 86
- A Glass of Wine 89

Chapter 18: Sensory Techniques 90
- Sensory Doodle 91
- Sensory Eyes 91
- Sensory Hook up 92
- Sensory Walking 93
- Finger-Knitting 94
- Finger-Weaving 95
- Stimming 96

Chapter 19: Establishing Rapport 97
- Match & Mirror: Posture 98
- Match & Mirror: Gestures 98
- Match & Mirror: Breathing 99
- Matching Language Patterns 100

Chapter 20: Brain Waves 101

Chapter 21: Summary 103

Appendix A: Additional Resources 104

Appendix B: Additional Links 106

References 108

Preface

Waves—Not Spoons is an exciting look at personal energy management that goes far beyond Spoon Theory and other previous energy management models.

Unlike the "spoons" analogy which implies a fixed amount of available energy, the Waves-Not Spoons analogy accommodates variations in the intensity and duration of energy needs and availability.

Waves-Not Spoons reminds us that following expenditures of energy (or Social Energy), we may require a period of rest or recovery regardless of how many spoons we have in the back.

Most importantly, the wave analogy goes beyond merely tracking the energy we've used. It provides insight into how we might proactively manage our available energy and even intervene at the appropriate times.

———————

No doubt many of are familiar with spoon theory as coined by Christine Miserandino in her 2003 essay entitled "The Spoon Theory".

The basic premise of her analogy was that for each day we all have a limited amount of energy available to us. And we can represent this energy as a certain number of spoons.

As you use up your energy, you take away a spoon. When your spoons are all used up, you're done for the day.

There's no question that the Spoon Theory has brought new awareness to personal energy issues. It's provided a useful model for many folks, especially those with chronic illness, in helping to manage their daily activities.

It was working with my own clients at the Neuro-linguistic Learning Center that I first came upon Ms. Miserandino's Spoon Theory.

While I found the model interesting as a basic accommodation, it failed to provide an adequate foundation for the positive interventions we were implementing at the NLC.

It was in support of these interventions that I first began utilizing the analogy of Waves to help my clients better understand and address the important aspects of energy management. And to that end, I realized I preferred Waves—Not Spoons as my own energy analogy.

Introduction

It was Monday morning and Jeremy was NOT looking forward to this day.

He'd already had a long and busy weekend and his sleep had been restless. He was scheduled for two staff meetings and a presentation all in the same day.

After hitting the snooze button twice in the hopes of getting another 30 minutes of sleep, Jeremy was already stressed and running late.

He grabbed a bagel with cream cheese and a cup of coffee for breakfast and headed out the door.

Since he was running late, Jeremy knew he'd be hitting traffic on the way to work.

His mind was racing as he looked for openings in the flow of traffic and rehearsed various conversations where he explained why he was late.

Jeremy was convinced that several drivers looked at him 'funny' as he and they jockeyed for positions in the stop and go traffic.

By the time Jeremy arrived at work, he felt he had already used up at least one of his spoons for the day.

After dropping his papers and laptop on his desk, Jeremy went straight to the employee break room and grabbed a doughnut and a cup of coffee.

Jeremy returned to his desk to check his email and voicemail before the morning staff meeting.

Jeremy tried replying to one of the emails but was still unsettled from the drive in so he wound up saving the email as a draft and went to reviewing his presentation for last minute changed.

Through the entire staff meeting Jeremy was distracted and stressed about his upcoming presentation. Jeremy was certain he used up another spoon.

By all standards, Jeremy's presentation went well. Most of the persons attending his presentation were completely unaware of Jeremy's nervousness.

Yet, despite his success, Jeremy left the meeting unsure of himself and anticipating negative feedback.

Jeremy was not comfortable being the center of attention and by the end of the presentation, Jeremy was mentally exhausted. He was sure he'd used up at least 2 more of his spoons' for the day.

Feeling like he had more to do than time to do it, Jeremy nervously ate lunch at his desk while replying to email and rehearsing what he and others would say at his next meeting.

Rather than coming back recharged by lunch, Jeremy felt more like he'd used up another spoon.

Jeremy's second meeting went much like the first. Jeremy fidgeted with his pencil, paper, his chair, and coffee cup through the entire meeting. His attention wandered and he struggled to stay engaged—another spoon.

By the time, Jeremy arrived back home he was thoroughly exhausted. In his mind he had absolutely no spoons left for the day.

He collapsed in front of the television and spoke little to his wife and kids for the rest of the evening.

Chapter 1: Understanding Waves

Simply put, waves represent the flow of energy—energy in and energy out. Waves may represent virtually any type of energy.

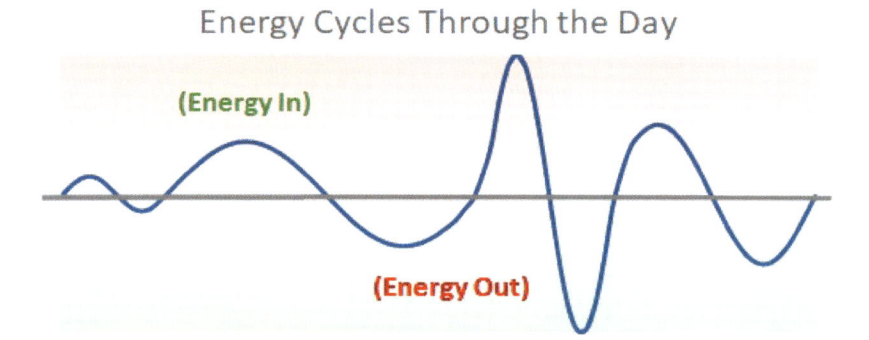

Energy Cycles Through the Day

(Energy In)

(Energy Out)

In this text, we will describe a number of wave-based strategies for managing our physical energy, our emotional energy, and our social

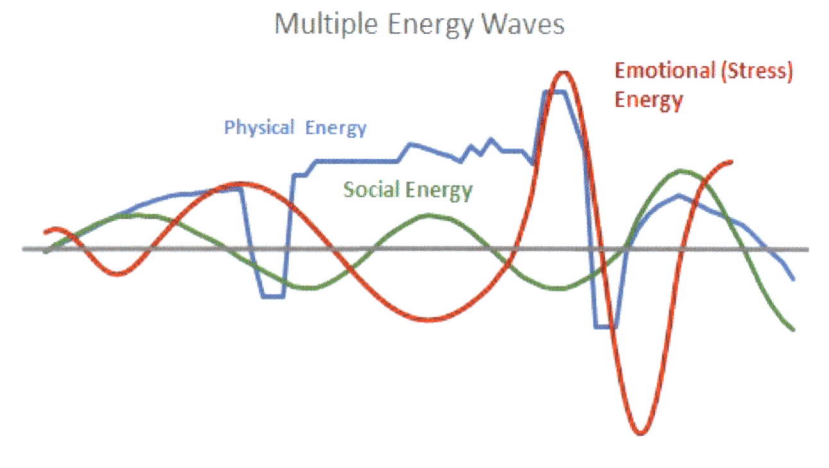

Multiple Energy Waves

Emotional (Stress) Energy

Physical Energy

Social Energy

energy.

A person's day may include multiple waves of various durations and intensities.

Short and Long Energy Cycles

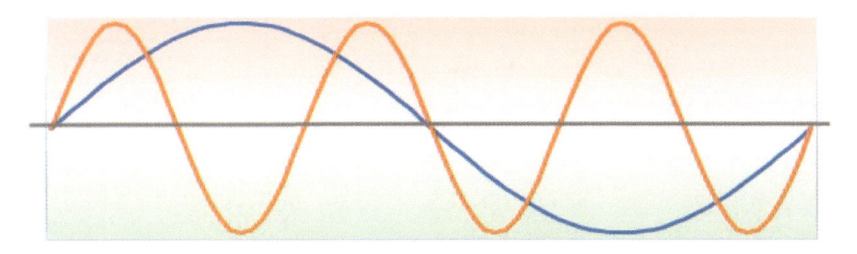

An important aspect of energy management is the need for rest and recovery.

Unlike spoon theory which simply counts the number of spoons used, Waves--Not Spoons reminds us that whenever spoons (energy) are used, there must be a commensurate period of rest and recovery.

This is analogous to running a sprint race vs. a marathon. The rest and recovery required for a sprint race may be a few minutes while the rest and recovery for a marathon may be several days.

The greater and longer the expenditure of energy, the greater or longer the need for rest and recovery.

In the following chapters, we'll present practical strategies for making the most of our periods of rest and recovery.

Chapter 2: Understanding Ourselves

In this chapter, we will lay the foundation for our individual application of Waves—Not Spoons by examining how we perceive and process sensory information.

There are four brain functions which, for the most part, determine how we perceive, process sensory information--our sensory profile.

Armed with an understanding of our sensory profile and our neurological strengths and weaknesses, we can more effectively support our values and goals as we move toward becoming fully self-expressed human beings.

• Dominant Brain Functions

What exactly do we mean by "dominant brain functions"?

Simply put, our dominant brain functions are those neurological functions which develop faster or stronger that other brain functions.

Research shows this development is typically a combination of two factors: nature, our genetic makeup; and nurture, our physical and emotional environment, especially childhood.

Think of it this way: every person is conceived/born with a certain personality based largely on their genetics. For discussion, let's call this our neurological personality.

As we grow, we will invariably have experiences—emotional, and environmental—which will influence the development of our neurological personality.

It is this combination of nature and nurture that has a profound effect on how the brain develops and specifically which brain functions develop faster or stronger than others.

For convenience, we will refer to these four primary brain functions as our FACE Personality: Feeling, Access, Consideration, and Excitement.

- **Flow of Sensory Information**

The following chart illustrates the flow of sensory information: what we see, hear, taste, smell, and touch, and how it is perceived and processed through a series of brain functions and, ultimately, our behavior.

Flow of Information

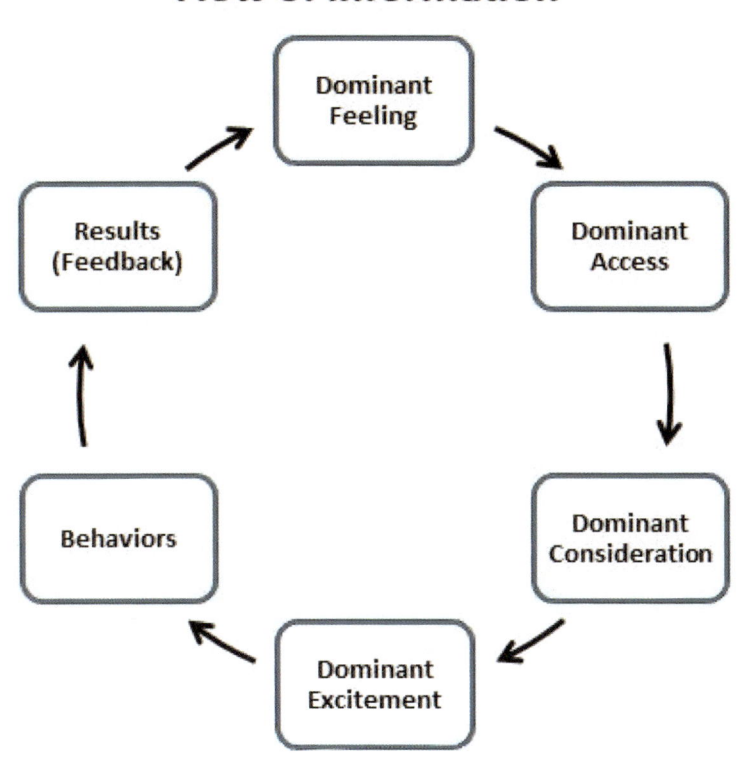

Dominant Feeling → Dominant Access → Dominant Consideration → Dominant Excitement → Behaviors → Results (Feedback) → Dominant Feeling

As we see in this graphic, the first step in the flow of sensory information is our **Dominant Feeling.** How we feel provides the context or filter through which we will perceive all sensory information.

The second step in the flow of sensory information is our **Dominant Access**. How we access sensory information is critical to our overall perception, organization, and storage of information.

The third step in the flow of sensory information is our **Dominant Consideration**. This function determines how we evaluate sensory information and is a critical component to the decision-making process.

The fourth step in the flow of sensory information is our **Dominant Excitement.** Our level of excitement determines how we respond neurologically to sensory information.

The results of all this filtering, sorting, processing, and storing, are our thoughts, feelings and behaviors. What most experts would call our personality.

Again, our four fundamental brain functions are:

- **Feeling (Sympathetic vs. Parasympathetic)**
- **Access (Visual vs. Auditory)**
- **Consideration (Logical vs. Emotional)**
- **Excitement (Over-Stimulated vs. Under-Stimulated)**

It is the dominance of these four neurological functions that determine how we perceive and process sensory information. Together these four dominant functions make up our sensory profile.

And it is this sensory profile that makes up our neurological personality or what we like to call our FACE Personality—Feeling, Access, Consideration and Excitement.

In this chapter, we'll briefly look at each of these four functions and how they effect our personality, our strengths, and our weaknesses.

- Dominant Feeling

In the FACE Personality Model, the first dominant brain function is, Feeling. This function has two possible states or traits: **sympathetic dominant** and **parasympathetic dominant**.

Sympathetic State (sympathetic dominance)	Parasympathetic State (parasympathetic dominance)
The sympathetic state and sympathetic dominance is a personality trait that often bears closer inspection as it can be the result of either neurology or trauma. Sympathetic Dominant persons may be hyper-alert to their surroundings. They may be highly reactive and may struggle with relationships, impulsivity, insomnia, organization, reading, writing, and memorization (particularly memory of auditory information, both written and verbal). Later in life, some sympathetic dominant persons may struggle with addiction and/or alcoholism.	The parasympathetic state and parasympathetic dominance is characterized by a more relaxed and more focused demeanor. Parasympathetic dominant persons tend to be responsive rather than reactive. They tend to do well in a typical classroom environment with a standard curriculum. They typically adapt well to standard reading and writing programs. Parasympathetic dominant persons tend to be well organized, with satisfactory memory for auditory information (both written and verbal).

Sympathetic dominant people are more reactive and can be either hyper-alert to their surroundings or hyper-focused.

When hyper-alert, they may have difficulty maintaining focus and attention. They may struggle with remembering written or spoken information.

Conversely, when hyper-focused, they may seem oblivious to their surroundings.

They may have trouble switching to new tasks and may become frustrated or react rudely if interrupted.

Sympathetic dominant people tend to be more alert to their surroundings. As a group, they're more active and physically fit.

However, if their stress and anxiety get the better of them, they can become overweight.

Sympathetic dominance is a personality trait that often bears closer inspection. One important question is whether the sympathetic dominance is the result of neurology or trauma.

If the dominance is neurological, there are skills and strategies we can learn to mitigate our stress response and improve our effectiveness and results.

However, if the dominance is the result of past trauma, it may justify the need for psychotherapy to address and resolve the past so that we can achieve better results in the present.

In some cases, extremely sympathetic dominant people may struggle with relationships, impulsivity, sleep, addiction and/or alcoholism.

In contrast, those persons who are parasympathetic dominant are generally more relaxed and less stressed than those who are sympathetic dominant.

Parasympathetic dominant persons tend to be more focused and more comfortable sitting for long periods of time.

They're more thoughtful and unless excited or stressed, are generally more responsive rather than reactive.

• Dominant Access

In our FACE Personality Model, the second dominant brain function is **Access.** This function has two possible states or traits: **visual** or **visual-spatial** and **auditory** or **auditory-verbal**.

Visually Dominant persons are generally intelligent, creative, inventive, non-linear, outside-the-box thinkers.

Visually dominant persons are frequently musical and/or artistic. They tend to organize information by patterns and associations rather than characteristics and features.

Auditory Dominant (Left-Brain)	**Visually Dominant** (Right-Brain)
Strengths: processing written and verbal information, linear thinking, order and sequence, perceiving features and characteristics, responsive. **Weaknesses:** creative thinking, abstract thinking, Intuitive thinking, pattern recognition	**Strengths:** visual-spatial acuity, creative thinking, non-linear thinking, intuitive thinking, pattern recognition, reactive, musical, artistic. **Weaknesses:** order and sequence, following instructions, processing written and Verbal information.

Some Visually Dominant people may struggle with organization, completing projects, being on time and maintaining even a simple schedule.

Those who are extremely sympathetic dominant and visually dominant may struggle with one or more symptoms of dyslexia, ADHD, and/or autism.

Conversely, Auditory Dominant people process information sequentially. They are generally highly organized and tend to start what they finish.

They are generally good listeners and storytellers and often have a strong sense of order and sequence and enjoy being on time.

• Dominant Consideration

The third dominant brain function in the FACE Personality Model is **Consideration**. This function has two possible states or traits: **logically**

Dominant Logical	Dominant Emotional
Strengths: logic and reason, critical thinking, literal, mis-matcher, sees differences. Dissociates from feelings.	Strengths: empathy, emotion, inferential thinking, matching, sees sameness. Associates into feelings.
Weaknesses: inferential thinking, empathy	Weaknesses: critical thinking, literal thinking

dominant and **emotionally dominant.**

People who are logically dominant are more likely to evaluate information and make decisions based on logic and reason and for them, rational thinking comes naturally.

Logically dominant people are typically comfortable taking the opposite view and may be prone to argue.

They may tend to dissociate from their own emotions (as well as the emotions of others) and may struggle with intimacy and a lack of empathy.

Because logically dominant persons tend to evaluate sensory information logically, they often have a strong sense of justice.

Conversely, people who are emotionally dominant tend to base their decisions on emotions and feelings.

Emotionally dominant people will naturally associate into their emotions and typically have a strong sense of empathy for others if they are not overwhelmed by their sensitivity.

They typically make friends easily and naturally enter rapport with others.

• Dominant Excitement

The fourth brain function in the FACE Personality Model is **Excitement**. This function has two possible states or traits: under-stimulated and over-

Dominant Under-Stimulated	Dominant Over-Stimulated
Typically an extravert, likes parties. Is easily bored. Generally enjoys large groups, concerts, and events.	Easily over-stimulated, likely to be introvert, may avoid large groups, gatherings, and parties.
May struggle with focus and attention one-on-one or in quiet settings.	May struggle with feeling overwhelmed in group settings, including typical classroom.
Needs action, chaos. Can become adrenaline-junky or thrill-seeker.	Probably prefers the quiet life and needs some alone time to 'recharge'.

stimulated.

Dominant under-stimulated people tend to be stimulation seekers.

They typically enjoy action and excitement and may become easily bored.

Dominant under-stimulated are generally extrovert, enjoying loud parties and large events.

Conversely, dominant over-stimulated people are typically stimulation avoiders.

These persons may be easily over-stimulated and may avoid loud parties and large events.

Those who are dominant over-stimulated are frequently more introverted in their behavior and/or may be naturally shy.

• Dominant—NOT Exclusive

It is vitally important to remember that these personality traits are not exclusive.

We are all a combination of BOTH our dominant traits AND our non-dominant traits.

However, these dominant traits have a profound influence on our strengths and weaknesses.

With this information, we can more easily identify and predict when and where we will be expending more of our energy as well as how we might best recharge our batteries when needed.

The NLC book, "What Personality Type Am I? A Brain-Based Guide to Personality and Relationships" describes each of the 16 neurological personalities in detail and includes a Personality Assessment based on the FACE Personality Model.

Chapter 3: Personal Waves

Once we understand our strengths and weaknesses (how we perceive and process sensory information), we're in a much better place to assess how best to manage our physical, emotional, and social energy waves.

Some folks will have a greater need to actively manage their physical energy more than others just to "get through the day".

Others may need to more actively manage their time or energy related to their personal relationships and social interactions.

And for still others, managing their emotional energy and dealing with emotional issues such as depression, anxiety or stress will be the greater challenge.

As we work our way down from the more general/conceptual information, we will arrive at specific strategies and techniques for managing these different areas of our lives.

In addressing our physical, emotional and social energy, two important elements which deserve our attention are rhythm and routine.

• Rhythm Waves

As human beings, much of our lives revolve around daily, weekly, monthly, and even yearly cycles. These cycles provide a rhythm to many of our activities.

There are also hidden cycles. The main human cycles are the 24-hour **circadian rhythms** that help regulate our sleep -wake cycle.

The **diurnal rhythms** that synchronize our metabolic functions today and night.

The **ultradian rhythms** govern our levels of alertness throughout the day and the cycle s of brain activity when we're asleep.

Infradian rhythms are biological rhythms that last more than 24 hours. The menstrual cycle and Seasonal Affective Disorder are examples of infradian rhythms.

These rhythms help regulate our alertness, hormone levels, sleep cycle, blood pressure, body temperature, decision-making, and more.

However, even with these natural rhythms as a backdrop, much of our lives can feel disordered and even in conflict with these natural rhythms.

While many folks naturally associate into these rhythms and live much of their lives in 'harmony', many others struggle to maintain any sense of rhythm and routine in their lives.

• Routine Waves

There are also those who perceive routines as a restriction or inconvenience.

Finally, there are many people who, for a variety of circumstances or commitments (school, career, etc.) find themselves in conflict with their natural rhythms.

In addition to managing our available energies, routines can also help us tune in and utilize our natural rhythms.

It's important distinction between schedules and routines. We create schedules to organize our tasks on time. Schedules are by definition artificial and are generally a response or solution to external considerations. Schedules may not correlate to any of our natural rhythms or needs.

We create routines to accommodate our natural rhythms, including our physical, sensory, and emotional needs. The Waves model is the tool to bring our external considerations and commitments into alignment with our natural rhythms.

Does the Waves model suggest ignoring our responsibilities and commitments? No! Absolutely not.

The Waves is a tool to *help* us keep our responsibilities and commitments while *also* honoring our physical, sensory, and emotional needs.

It is specifically for this reason that we need to nourish a greater understanding and awareness of those needs.

It is also important that we develop willingness, commitment, and flexibility to stop when necessary in order to honor our physical, sensory, and emotional needs.

• Chronic Illness

Some persons, particularly those struggling with the effects of chronic illnesses, may have difficulty acquiring energy (spoons) and may expend their available energy more quickly.

While it should go without saying, we must not judge ourselves or compare ourselves to others.

When we accept ourselves for who we are and what we have to offer we are in the best position to make the most of our strengths and accommodate our weaknesses when needed.

It is also important to repeat that this is not a medical text and medical issues including but not limited to crone's disease, fibromyalgia, lupus, lime disease, etc., are beyond the scope of this text.

Physical injuries, chronic illness and disabilities are beyond the scope of this text.

Always seek the advice of a medical professional if you suspect any medical issue or before making any changes to your exercise or dietary routines.

Whatever our challenges, our greatest success and effectiveness will come by managing our day to include those essential periods of rest and recover.

• Chronic Pain

As with chronic illness, chronic pain is a medical issue and, unfortunately, beyond the scope of this text.

What can be said here is that, like chronic illness, chronic pain is real and cannot simply be ignored or wished away. Some basic strategies for helping chronic pain are outlined in chapters 16, 17 and 20, including stress reduction, massage, guided imagery, brain entrainment, and acupuncture.

One important strategy for living with chronic illness and chronic pain is to connect with other folks living with similar struggles.

Try to seek out folks who are not merely suffering with their illness but finding solutions and strategies for making their lives better.

• Wholistic Approach

It goes without saying that a book of this nature cannot possibly encompass or predict that issues that every individual may face. Our hope is to bring awareness to some of the issues that underly and effect our available physical, emotional and social energies.

And as we each develop a more complete picture of these available energies, we are in a much better place to proactively address our individual needs as we become more fully self-expressed human beings.

Chapter 4: Physical Energy Waves

In this chapter we'll focus on our physical energy and the differences between the "Spoons Theory" and the "Waves—Not Spoons" Model.

The first thing to keep in mind is that energy is always flowing in and out. We are continuously either expending energy (out) or recharging our energy stores (in).

This understanding tells us that under the right conditions we can recharge our (energy) batteries, not just at night when we're asleep, but anytime during the day or night.

While we may start our day with a given amount of energy (spoons), we can actually add energy (spoons) throughout our day.

High & Low Energy Waves

Energy Out — High Energy Flow — Moderate Energy Flow — Low Energy Flow — Energy In

The second thing to keep in mind is that energy may be expended slower over a longer period of time (cycle) or faster over a shorter cycle.

Just as we can measure energy consumed in calories per hour, we could measure our personal energy consumption in spoons per hour.

As we also see in our graphic, a longer cycle of energy out will typically require a longer recovery period while the shorter cycle (sprinters) may require shorter and more frequent recover periods.

An understanding and awareness of our personal energy cycles as discussed in Chapter 3 can help us determine how best to use and recover our personal energy and thereby plan accordingly.

For example, some folks may do best with shorter, more intense energy cycles (sprinters).

They may need to eat and rest more often, perhaps every 45 to 90 minutes.

Conversely, others may find they perform better if they maintain lower energy intensity over longer periods of time (marathoner).

They may require extended periods of rest and larger less frequent meals.

Furthermore, when we notice a significant change in our energy cycles, it may be that something has changed, and we need to adjust our schedule.

The important point is that these individual preferences will almost always occur as patterns that we can map out and integrate into our daily lives as rhythms and routines.

Rather than reacting to our energy needs, we can more effectively plan to meet those needs proactively.

Imagine a piece of tempered steel. We can bend that piece over and over and over again and it will (for all practical purposes) return to its original shape... over and over and over again.

But we can do this ONLY as long as we do not exceed to point of failure.

Once the point of failure is exceeded, that object is damaged and will NOT return to its original shape. The piece must be re-forged and re-tempered before it can be re-used.

As people, we are far more effective when we can push ourselves without exceeding the point of failure. In this same way, 5, 10, or even 20 small results are far better in the long run than one massive project that ultimately exceeds the point of failure.

Chapter 5: Emotional Energy Waves

For some persons it's not unusual to find themselves in challenging or stressful situations multiple times in a single day. It may be the drive to work, a presentation or just a phone call.

The important thing to recognize is that ANY event is potentially stressful.

Also important is the realization that the stress from one event can linger or bleed over into other events, sometimes with negative if not disastrous consequences.

Increasing Stress throughout the Day

While a relaxed and focused state of mind may come easily to most people, some people, especially those who are sympathetic dominant and those diagnosed with ADHD may struggle with achieving a relaxed state of mind.

Most human beings will naturally slip in and out of a relaxed state of mind several times a day, typically. It is a state of mind that everyone is capable of achieving under the right circumstances.

The question is when and how do we achieve this important state?

As it happens, each of us has a built-in "switch", a neurological button, that enables us to switch from a stressed and anxious state to a relaxed and focused state.

In our physical and emotional exercises, we will exploit this neurological switch.

• The Autonomic Nervous System

This switch is part of our Autonomic Nervous System (ANS). The ANS controls the autonomic or automatic functions in our body. Growth, healing, digestion, pupil dilation, respiration, heart rate, adrenalin, situational awareness, problem-solving, release of adrenalin, reflexes and reactivity are just some of the systems and functions influenced by the ANS.

Autonomic Nervous System (ANS)

Sympathetic Nervous System	Parasympathetic Nervous System
(Fight-or-Flight)	(Rest and Digest)
Fear, Anger, Stress (Anxiety, Depression)	Learning State Happy, Content, Joy
Perception Dominant (hyper-alert)	Judgment Dominant (thoughtful)
Utilize (react to) Sensory Information	Store and Recall Sensory Information
Binocular (Foveal) Vision	Peripheral Vision
Increased Blood to Muscles Digestion Slows Healing Slows Growth Slows	Rest and Sleep Digestion Healing Growth

The ANS begins in the hypothalamus. For simplicity, we'll divide the Autonomic Nervous System (ANS) into two major systems: the **Sympathetic Nervous System** and the **Parasympathetic Nervous System**. These two seemingly redundant systems are connected to virtually every muscle and organ in the human body.

It's no wonder the Autonomic Nervous System (ANS) has a profound effect on our physiology and our behavior.

When our sympathetic nervous system is activated—when we are in the 'fight or flight' state—our perception and visual-spatial (situational) awareness becomes heightened. Our focus is directed towards the external. Our intuitive, creative, visual-spatial thinking is directed to surviving whatever is happening in the present moment.

Conversely, when our Parasympathetic Nervous System is activated—when we are in a relaxed and focused state—our thought processes tend to be more introspective and reflexive.

Rather than simply reacting to our current situation, we are far more likely to be comfortable as observers, passively taking in and store information. Instead of problem-solving for survival, our visual-spatial thoughts are free to form eidetic memories (pictures and movies) and to integrate these new memories with existing memories.

It goes without saying that the state of our ANS has a profound effect on our ability to perceive and store information. Therefore, our ability to perceive and retain any verbal information, either written or auditory.

The good news is thanks to the research conducted at the Neuro-linguistic Learning Center, we've developed simple exercises to switch our ANS from the sympathetic state to the parasympathetic state.

This internal switch helps us turn off our hyper-alert, puzzle-solving state and turn on our relaxed and focused, record and playback state.

These techniques are outlined in Chapter 17: Emotional Energy Refresh Techniques, *Chapter 18: Sensory Techniques, and Chapter 19: Brain Waves.*

The amazing thing is that in just minutes, these simple exercises can help shift a person's physical and mental state so that our reading experience is not only more effective, but more enjoyable.

Chapter 6: Social Energy Waves

As a very general rule, the expenditure of social 'energy' often comes down to how comfortable you are in a given situation.

The more comfortable you are, the longer your social energy will last. The less comfortable you are with a given person or event, the faster you will deplete your social energy reserve.

The keys to being comfortable with interpersonal or social engagements is rapport. It's a simple formula: **Rapport = Comfort**

The more we're in rapport, the greater the level of comfort. The less rapport, the lower the level of comfort.

It follows that establishing rapport, be it with one person or many, is where we want to 'invest' our social energy.

Social Energy Waves

- Social Events (Energy Out)
- Public Speaking
- Group Events
- Relationships
- Alone Time (Energy In)

I should point out that there are persons who are naturally able to establish rapport more easily than others.

These persons will generally feel more comfortable in some social situations such that their social energy batteries actually recharge when they attend social engagements. It's as if their batteries feed off the emotional energy in the room.

For many of us, however, interpersonal and social events require us to expend our social energy to create that level of rapport and comfort.

Additionally, some persons struggle with additional issues such as social anxiety, autism and PTSD. These issues can make correctly reading complex and/or conflicting social cues, dealing with sensory overload, and/or filtering through a mix of overlapping conversations significantly more difficult.

We have included an array of stress reduction and sensory exercises as well as a variety of techniques for:

- Creating empathy and rapport
- Making small talk and chit-chat
- Speaking and Listening
- Dealing family dynamics
- Reading social events
- Educational skills for school
- Special skills for job/career.

As with our physical and emotional Energy, we want to practice <u>conservation of energy</u> in our interpersonal and social relationships in three ways:

1) We want to begin our days and events with as much social energy in our batteries as possible.
2) We want to avoid wasting our social energy on fear, anger, stress, anxiety and guilt.
3) We want to recharge our social energy batteries as often as possible.

Every person will respond to interpersonal and social events differently. And, as we saw in the previous graph, most people will expend more social energy speaking in public and attending group events than they will in private, personal relationships.

Waves—Not Spoons is all about understanding your personal energies and how those energies are used.

Chapter 7: Relationship Waves

> *"**No man is an Island**, entire of itself..."* - Thomas Merton

Relationships are a key aspect of life; some even argue, the most important aspect.

That said, there's no question that the dynamics of relationships could easily be described as complex, confusing, and even challenging.

For some folks, the demands of maintaining healthy relationships can be overwhelming, and for all these reasons, we've developed some basic strategies for developing and sustaining healthy relationships.

The first and most obvious wave strategy is to address the issue of relationship energy drain.

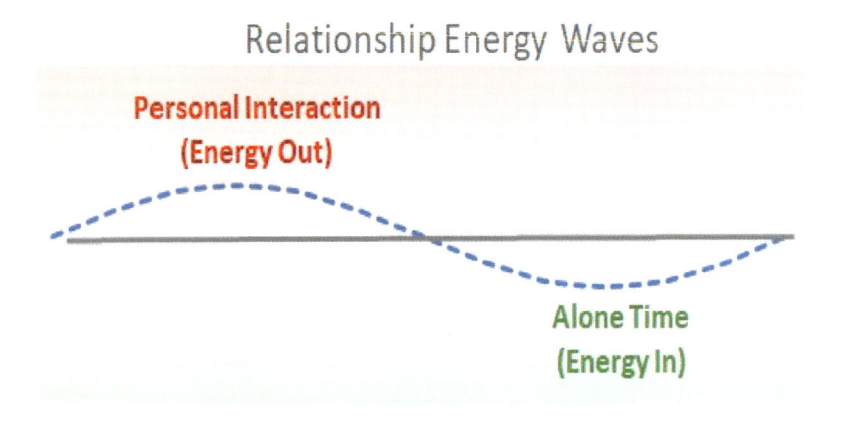

Relationship Energy Waves

Personal Interaction (Energy Out)

Alone Time (Energy In)

The fact is, establishing rapport, dealing with different communication styles, reading social cues, and managing the ebb and flow of conversation, all while having meaningful and respectful dialogue, requires us to maintain our focus and attention.

While some persons can maintain that level of focus and attention more easily that others, NO ONE can maintain that state indefinitely.

Sooner or later, EVERYONE needs a break. Everyone needs some alone time. With Waves—Not Spoons, we want to make the most of that alone time to recharge our batteries.

At one time or another, be it in a long-term relationship or a casual conversation, most of us have felt some form of energy drain be it in the form of feeling overwhelmed, smothered, drained, suffocated, stifled, detached, dissociated or confused.

All of these can be a sign that we need to step back and take time to recharge our relationship batteries.

Depending on our dominant personality traits and those of our friends, family, or partners, our relationships may be more or less energy intensive.

It is also a reality that some people are 'energy intensive'. That is, they seem to require more effort or energy to maintain a healthy relationship.

There are those, too, who seem to 'suck the life' out of those around them. These people may warrant limited exposure and, if necessary, removal from our life altogether.

As we spend less time tired, anxious, angry and stressed, we are more likely to become aware and observant of our own emotional energy flow.

We may find that when we are with some people, we tend to feel drained of our energy while in the company of others, we feel refreshed and renewed.

As we move forward with our new awareness and new skills, we may find ourselves setting new boundaries and even new goals for ourselves and our relationships.

> ***Remember: even GOOD people can have BAD relationships.***

Once again, when we look at our relationships, it is important to do so WITHOUT judgement.

It's possible for two good people to not get along. It's possible for people to have good intentions, even to care for each other, but not have the temperament or skills to form a healthy relationship.

• Masking

Masking is most often associated with Autism and Autism Spectrum Disorders.

Masking might be described as suppressing our true feelings and sensory perceptions so that we can pretend to look and feel normal. It is, literally, putting on a good face, in spite of feelings and perceptions to the contrary.

Masking creates a false impression as it conceals the masking person's true feelings and perceptions. It reinforces the feeling of isolation for the person masking. And it supports the mistaken belief that the person masking cannot be accepted for who and what he is.

Similar to other imposed or trained behaviors (imposed by self or others), to the extent that masking conflicts with our feelings and sensory perception, it undermines a person's self-esteem, confidence and empathy. Ultimately, it impairs people's ability to trust themselves and their perceptions.

Sadly, there are psychologists and therapist who actually promote masking and masking-like behaviors as appropriate therapy.

From our perspective, teaching and promoting masking is rarely effective and has too many long term negative side effects to EVER be considered an appropriate therapy.

Effective therapy is about learning who we are—our strengths and weaknesses and providing the tools to become emotionally fulfilled and fully self-expressed human beings.

And in the domain of self-expression, we can also acquire skills and strategies to help us more effectively find success however we define it.

- **Impostor Syndrome**

Pretending to be something we're not is, essentially, a lighter, less intensive form of masking.

While it may not rise to the same level of sensory conflict as masking, pretending to be someone we're not frequently results in many of the same side effects and consequences as masking.

When the pretending becomes an obsessive or compulsive behavior, it is referred to as Imposter Syndrome.

- **People Pleasers**

At first glance, people pleasing may seems like a good thing, especially to those on the receiving end.

We might be inclined to think that as long as no one gets hurt, people pleasing is a win-win with everyone getting what they want.

But like pretending and masking, the pleaser is sacrificing their own feelings and sensory needs for the sake of a false image or narrative. In so doing, they eventually harm themselves as well as the relationship.

To be clear, does this mean we can't be nice to people or go out of our way to support others just because we're tired in the moment or because a particular supportive action is "not really our thing"?

No, not at all. As part of being the best expression of who we are we can at times subordinate our immediate gratification or a particular desire in support of our partner or the relationship.

To be clear, this is not masking, people pleasing or pretending to be someone we are not in so much as we are free to offer or not offer the support.

• Abusive Relationships

> *"Beauty is in the eye of the beholder... and so is abuse."*

In any relationship, it is the absolute right of each person to decide and determine what is and is not abusive behavior.

It does not matter what is "normal". It does not matter what any other person thinks or feels.

If a person feels that a particular behavior directly towards them is abusive then by definition that behavior is abusive. And it is the absolute right and the responsibility of that person to reject that behavior and to communicate that rejection, that boundary, as clearly and as forcefully as necessary.

It is the responsibility of all persons in relationship to respect the other person's boundaries. No one has the right to reject or 'step over' another person's boundaries excepting to defend themselves or others again harm.

We will avoid going too far afield on this issue except to say that it is NOT OK to violate another person's boundaries simply because someone is of the opinion they seem 'over-sensitive' or even unreasonable.

Everyone is entitled to define their own boundaries. Everyone is entitled to mutual respect. And everyone has the right to walk away from a relationship.

It's also useful to remember that rejecting a person's behavior is NOT the same as rejecting the person. We are NOT our behaviors.

We may care for another person. We may have love and compassion for another person. And that person may have the best of intentions.

It does not necessarily follow that we will have an intimate, lasting or healthy relationship with that person.

Personalities vary widely. Goals and Values vary widely. There are very good people who simply don't get along with each other and that is OK!

Chapter 8: Communication Waves

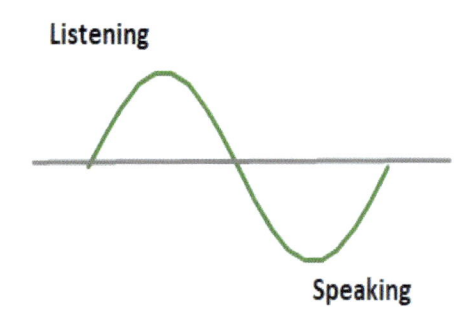

Communication is like a dance. It requires the participation of both parties. It requires focus and attention. And, as we discussed in previous chapters, it requires energy.

For our purposes, the basic communication wave is made up of speaking and listening. As a social convention, it is typically appropriate for the speaking and listening to be relatively balanced.

While this may seem obvious, it is all too common for conversations to be dominated by one person.

In some cases, a one-sided conversation is intentional and fills a need expressed by one or both parties.

At other times, a one-sided conversation may simply be due to a lack of awareness on the part of one or both parties.

If a person compulsively feels the need to dominate the conversation or be the center of attention, this may be a sign of past negative experiences, low self-esteem or an insecurity that warrants further attention.

Conversely, if a person finds himself unable to actively participate in a conversation or compulsively avoids being seen as the center of attention, this may also be a sign of past negative experiences, low self-esteem or an insecurity that warrants further attention.

That said, if the issue is simply a lack of awareness then creating new healthy communication habits should go a long way to balancing out the dance.

It should be noted that strong emotions, like stress, anxiety, anger, and even excitement, can interfere with that awareness. The more relaxed and focused we are, the more likely we are to maintain our awareness.

In addition to exercising awareness, there are some basic communication skills that anyone can use to improve their communication effectiveness.

While strictly speaking these are not part of the Waves Model, we've included them along with other exercises to support our readers.

• Communication Styles

In previous chapters, we looked at people's personalities and how they perceive and process sensory information.

As one would expect, it is natural for people's speaking and listening to reflect their personalities and how they perceive and process information.

We might call this speaking and listening their communication style. And it is not uncommon for two people with different personalities to have very different communication styles.

For example, folks who are visually dominant may tend to speak and respond to words and phrases that reflect their visual dominance. "Can you see/picture…" or "It's clear to me," are just a few phrases a visually dominant person might use.

Conversely, auditory dominant persons may respond to phrases like, "I hear/heard you" or "It sounds good to me".

Those of us who are logically dominant may tend to use phrases like, "It makes sense to me" or "That seems logical".

While feeling/emotionally dominant folks may say, "It feels like..." or "I would love to...".

Without awareness, it is absolutely possible for two people to speak and hear the same word but have a completely different understanding due to differing communication styles.

The following graph is a tongue-in-cheek look at what often happens when a Visual/Emotional Dominant (V/E) person tries to convey his or her excitement about something to an Auditory/Logical Dominant

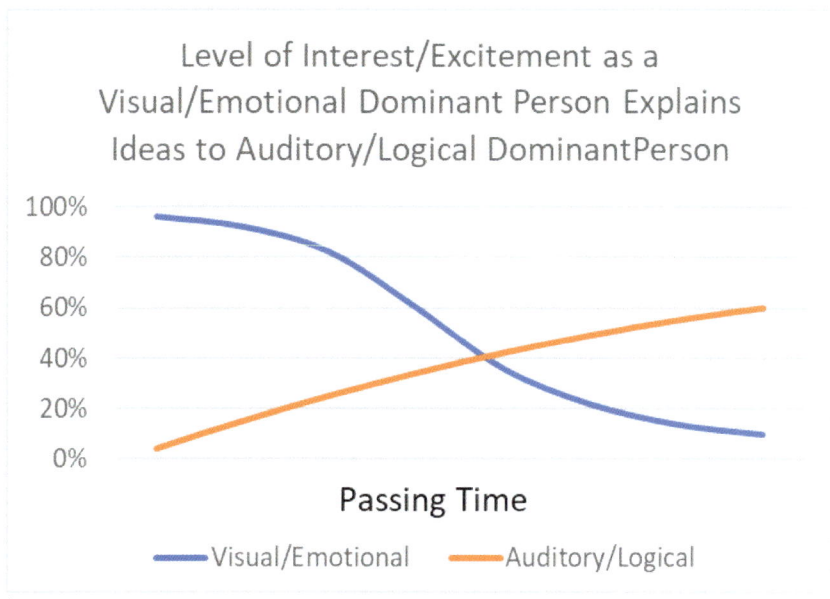

Level of Interest/Excitement as a Visual/Emotional Dominant Person Explains Ideas to Auditory/Logical Dominant Person

Passing Time

— Visual/Emotional   — Auditory/Logical

(A/L) person.

As you can see, the Visual/Emotional Dominant person starts out over-the-moon excited and wants to convey that excitement to the Auditory/Logical Dominant person. (This is a conversation that husbands and wives have re-played a million times.)

As the V/E person takes his conceptual, big picture vision and breaks it down into 'chunks' that the A/L person can digest, the V/E person's excitement begins to wane.

At some point, the A/L person may get excited about the idea but by that time, the V/E has often lost his own interest/excitement for the idea.

If we are not consciously looking at our own communication style as well as those of our audience, we may be misunderstanding each other completely or at the very least, missing the opportunity to build empathy and rapport.

• Visual Communication

Visual Communication is a technique for making our discussions easier, more effective, and hopefully, more enjoyable.

However, there is no free lunch. As with any other skill, these techniques MUST BE PRACTICED in order to be effective.

The basic 'trick' of Visual Communication is that instead of relying solely on the 3% of our brain that processes verbal information, Visual Communication actively engages the 30% of our brain that processes Visual-Spatial information.

• Visual Listening

The important of being able to listen fully and attentively cannot be overestimated.

The entire premise of a meaningful conversation rests on each person's ability to listen to what the other person is saying and respond accordingly.

And the ability to listen effectively is, without question, contingent upon a person's ability to achieve and sustain focus and attention.

One sure way to help achieve that sustained focus and attention is NOT to focus on the speaker's words but instead focus on and VISUALIZE the meaning of what the other person is saying.

When we visualize what the other person is saying, we engage our visual cortex, a full 30% of our brain, in creating our eidetic images of what the person is saying.

We can make those images as engaging as possible with bright vivid colors and as much action and movement as necessary to keep our undivided attention.

Notice that it is NOT possible to create this level of engagement if we are simply focused on the words. Listening to and focusing on 3-4 words per second may hold some people's attention, but for many of us it will not.

On the other hand, visualizing the meaning of those same words can help hold the attention of even the most active mind.

And, not only does visual listening help hold our attention on what the other person is saying, it keeps our mind actively engaged in the making of conversation and far more likely to offer a meaningful response.

For those of us who struggle with attention issues, Visual Listening helps block out distractions and quiets that inner chatter in our own head.

With just a little practice Visual Listening can become your best friend in communication.

- ## Visual Speaking

At some point, it becomes our turn to speak. Now, what to say?

Unfortunately, if we've been distracted by everything around us or lost in a dialogue inside our own head, responding in any meaningful way may prove difficult to impossible.

One trap many folks fall into at one time or another is rehearsing what they're going to say while they're supposed to be listening to the other person speak.

While this tactic can sometimes create the illusion of listening, more often than not, the listener looks more like a racehorse at the starting gate just waiting for the other person to stop talking so he can speak.

Visual Listening helps us avoid this trap by deeply engaging us in what the other person is saying.

And when it does become our turn to speak, we are in a much better place to engage and respond appropriately and meaningfully.

This does beg the question: how will I find the right words to say (in the moment) if I don't rehearse it in my head?

We have two very easy answers to this important question.

The first answer is we don't listen to the WORDS. We listen for the MEANING.

Again, where do we find the meaning?

Answer: we find our meaning in our VISUALIZATION of what the other person said.

It's amazing, it's easy, and it's fast (30-40 eidetic images per second fast).

And when it is our turn to speak, simply look to the eidetic images we made while the other person was speaking and focus in on one or two items that grab our attention. THAT is what we talk about. That's what we say.

We keep your comments brief (one or two minutes) and limited to those one or two points.

We're almost done speaking but there's one more gift we can give the other person. We can finish what we're saying by ASKING them a question.

Yes! We make our point, express ourselves through our respectful and engaged listening and then we keep the conversation going by respectfully asking the other person for their thoughts.

Visual Speaking helps eliminate those desperate moments trying to figure out what we're going to say. It's all right there. Meaningful, engaging communication is right there on the tip of the tongue.

• Greetings

While, "Hi. How are you?" is the tried and true all-purpose greeting, the inevitable response, "Fine. How are you?" in its innumerable variations is always safe if a bit stale.

At 98% of all social events, never, never, never answer the question, "How are you?" with a litany of complaints, ailments, or the latest personal misfortunes. Trust me. It is a conversation killer and will leave you standing alone at the punch bowl.

Fortunately, there's a lot of room between "Fine" and a 20-minute dissertation on my irritable bowel syndrome.

A general statement like, "It's been a challenging week" or "I've decided I hate cars. How about you?" can let others know that things aren't perfect without inviting sympathy or making others feel confused and uncomfortable. At the same time, the "How about you?" invites the other person to engage.

Try to keep your greeting(s) short, simple and a little bit interesting.

"Hi. My name is Gerry. Mostly I help children with dyslexia learn to read and write. How about you?"

There's nothing wrong with a canned greeting. If you have your own business, and it feels appropriate, an entertaining 30-second "elevator speech" can be a real icebreaker.

"Hi. Gerry H. I'm Director of the Neuro-linguistic Learning Center. We work with children and teens to help take the stress and struggle out of learning. In reality, we mostly work with parents, so they save their kids from a mind-numbing education."

The trick is to open the door to an interesting dialogue without 'dumping'.

In greetings, a little goes a long way.

• Goodbyes

While greetings can seem awkward, goodbyes can feel even more awkward.

Oddly enough, a handshake and simple, "It was nice meeting you. I'm going to [find someone / do something]." is often a perfectly appropriate ending to a conversation at most social events.

At almost any business event, "Nice meeting you. Do you have a [business] card?" is a great way to end a brief meeting with someone new.

To that end, it is always good to carry your own business cards or even cards with your personal contact information so you if someone asks for your contact information you can hand them your card (rather than searching for your phone or a pen).

A final word on business cards, NEVER offer to give your business card unless someone asks for one. They will only wind up in the trash.

• Smalltalk and Chit-Chat

The first rule of communication is, "He who asks the questions, controls the conversation."

Rather than making yourself the center of attention by answering questions, let the other person be the center of attention by asking them questions.

One simple strategy is to grab a few current events or interesting topics off the news or twitter. After introductions, a segue into, "Did you see/hear about…?" or "What do you think about the…?" can get the conversation going.

Asking people for information or their opinion is always good for discussion.

You can ask people what they think about whatever is happening at the moment, i.e., "How do you like the play?" or "What did you think of [your favorite part of the movie]?".

You can ask if a person has ever been to a specific place, i.e., Disneyland, Yosemite, Alaska, etc.

Sex, politics, and religion are always dangerous topics, but with the right audience, an invitation to talk about the economy or a local political issue can be real conversation starter.

Note: We build rapport by finding common ground, but respectful discussion with some difference in perspective makes for much more interesting conversation.

Special interests can be great conversation starters and a place to share your expertise.

But be careful! The history of steam locomotives can become overwhelming really fast.

Eyes glazing over, furtive glances from side to side, pursed lips and lowering of the eyebrows are typically signs of boredom or lack of interest.

Speaking for myself only. Will I EVER be the life of the party? Probably not. But can I comfortably engage in a meaningful conversation without masking or pretending and enjoy just be myself? Absolutely.

- ## Empathy and Rapport

The previous tips are great for handling the mechanics of communication. But the true satisfaction and fulfillment in communication come from establishing empathy and rapport.

It should be noted that while achieving feelings of empathy comes easily to some, it can be challenging for others.

If we recall our sensory profiles, we see that Emotionally Dominant persons typically feel empathy for others more easily while Logically Dominant persons may struggle with empathy.

In addition, anger, stress, anxiety, and fear will interfere with our ability to feel empathetic towards others.

So, regardless of our sensory profile, the first ingredient to establishing empathy is a relaxed and focused state.

This is critical because when our Sympathetic (fight or flight) Nervous system is activated, our neurological reaction is to close ourselves off, to dissociate from our own emotions as well as the emotions of others.

If we, ourselves, are feeling anger, fear, or stress, those around us are far more likely to feel uncomfortable.

Conversely, when we are in the Parasympathetic State (relaxed and focused), those around us are far more likely to feel relaxed and at ease.

Therefore, our first goal is do everything we can to reduce stress in our daily lives in general and, specifically, before, during, and after personal interactions and social events.

In subsequent chapters, we describe in detail dozens of stress reduction strategies and exercises.

Our second goal is to establish rapport in the conversation. Rapport is an amazing and powerful phenomenon in which the physiological state of two or persons can actually synchronize.

Establishing a state of deep rapport virtually guarantees a more relaxed and focused state and opens the door to a profound empathy.

There are several well-established paths to establishing rapport.

1) The first is all about observing and sharing things you have in common.

2) The second path is to match and mirror your own physiology to the other person or persons.

3) The third path to establishing empathy and rapport is by association.

Each of these are discussed in detail in Chapter 19: Establishing Rapport.

Perhaps the most important take away is that all these skills can be learned. Learning to relax and focus is possible for all human beings. Establishing rapport is possible and natural for all human beings. Feeling empathy is a natural phenomenon for all human beings.

Remember that, learning any new skill can take time and practice. While some of this may seem complicated or overwhelming, taken slowly and one piece at a time, all these skills can be learned and with a success and repetition, become habit.

Finally, use the strategies and techniques and the knowledge of your own sensory profile to recharge your communication batteries as needed so you can more thoroughly participate in and enjoy all your communications and social interactions.

Chapter 9: Family Waves

As the saying goes, you can choose your friends, but you don't get to choose your family.

While this is true with respect to our genealogy, it does NOT govern our actions and who we choose to spend our time with.

As human beings, we are free to choose with whom we associate as well as how much we associate.

And while every choice has consequences, and some persons may find themselves in untenable situations through seemingly no fault of their own, ultimately, the choice to interact with others is our s and ours alone.

I say this NOT as a fact to be debated, but as a perspective from which to view our world.

I say this because the simple perspective that we are choosing our life has a degree of power and facilitates that relaxed and focused state.

Conversely, perceiving that we are helpless and/or trapped is far more likely to leave us feeling anxious, angry, and afraid.

We've already reviewed how a relaxed and focused state is the foundation for establishing empathy and rapport.

This is no more important than when communicating with family members with whom we are likely to have a lifelong relationship.

That said, we may or may not choose to open up and establish empathy and rapport with every member of our family.

We may also establish boundaries. We can choose how often or in what 'doses' we interact and communicate with some or all of our family members.

Holidays and family gatherings can be particularly challenging or stressful for some folks. It may be important to review boundaries prior to family gathering. As we've said several times, Trust your Feelings. Trust your gut.

Another key difference between communicating with family members is that there is almost always a strong common ground or sense of relatedness with family members.

This strong common ground can provide a solid basis for communication (empathy and rapport) or it can bring with it, baggage (anxiety, anger, fear) which can greatly interfere with communication, empathy, and rapport.

Another strong factor in family communication and relationships is association.

For better or worse, family member will often have preconceived ideas about other family members based on their familiar associations.

"*The apple doesn't fall far from the tree*," and, "*Like father, like son,*" are just a few examples of judging by association.

That leads us to matching and mirroring to establish empathy and rapport with family members.

Please do not underestimate the power of these techniques, again found in Chapter 19: Establishing Rapport.

One more saying that's applicable to family dynamics is, "*Familiarity breeds contempt.*"

Try keep old feelings and/or past mistakes from clouding the present.

If appropriate, be willing to forgive the shortcomings of others as well as those of yourself.

Under no circumstances should anyone allow any form of abuse, mental or physical to continue. However, in some cases, old wounds can be healed and overcome, with appropriate therapy when needed.

And again, give yourself the time you need to rest and recharge your communication batteries between personal interactions and family events.

Chapter 10: Waves in the Classroom

This application of Waves in the Classroom is based on research conducted at the Neuro-Linguistic Learning Center in Northern California from 2006 to 2018.

NLC students ranged in ages 5 to 54 years old. Their challenges have included ADHD, Autism Spectrum Disorders, Dyslexia, and other learning challenges.

For those Students experiencing significant struggles in the classroom, we strongly recommend additional NLC resources, see Appendix A: Additional Resources.

Here, we will focus on a few key strategies to reduce stress and increase focus and attention as a means for improving academic performance.

The first thing to keep in mind is that our education system has evolved to accommodate a very distinct subset of the population.

This subset is comprised of a broad but very specific type of thinking and intelligence.

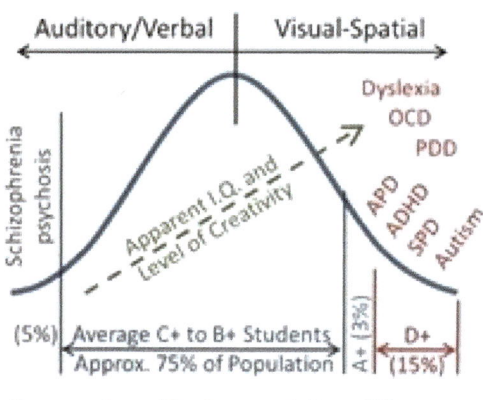

Learning Style and Intelligence

90% of all information in the classroom is presented verbally or written.

Information is organized by characteristics and features rather than patterns and applications.

Finally, almost all new concepts are taught by example (how) rather than by concept (why).

It is no surprise that only about 3% of all children truly excel in public school and only 65% of all children are successful (passing grades) in all subjects.

Approximately 20% of Kindergarten through High School students perform poorly in one or more subjects and as many as 15% are completely failing in most or all of their classes.

Given that the overall intelligence of 93% of school age children varies by less than 10% when developmental differences and other factors are taken into account, it is clear that the educational paradigm favors children with specific learning or sensory profile and is biased against many otherwise intelligent children but with a different sensory profile.

- Stress is the Enemy

Statistics show that only 60% of children and adults will naturally adapt to a standard education pedagogy and classroom pressures. Another 20% will adapt fairly well with assistance in one or more areas. The remaining 20% of adults and children, a standard educational curriculum and classroom environment will pose significant challenges.

The vast majority of these struggling children are extremely visually dominant in their Access (perception to sensory information). Many are also extremely emotionally dominant in their consideration (judgement/evaluation of sensory information).

To make matters worse, the sympathetic dominant neurology of children with Dyslexia and ADHD, can make sitting passively in a classroom difficult to near enough impossible.

Many of these visual learning children are highly intelligent and they often develop their own unique strategies to survive classroom life despite being the proverbial square peg in a round hole.

In addition to Sensory Exercises, like those in Chapter 18, providing frequent breaks during the school day, reasonable accommodations for test-taking, limits on class work and homework, quiet study time, unstructured play, exercise time, can greatly reduce a child's stress in the classroom.

Visual Learning strategies can help many students feel more connected to the teacher as well as the curriculum.

• Visual Learning State

Sitting comfortably in chair, focus on one spot well above eye level; hold for 20-30 slow breaths (one minute).

Expand your awareness to your peripheral vision while maintaining your focus on the spot.

After one minute, close both eyes and, looking slightly up and to the left, visualize a shiny red apple with two green leaves.

Hold the image of the apple steady for 30 seconds to one minute. (The supervising adult should repeat "visualize the shiny red apple… Hold it steady… Hold it… Shiny red apply with green leaves…").

To the image of the apple, add the word, "apple" in blue letters.

Again, hold the image of the apple together with the word, 'apple', for 30 seconds.

Repeat this exercise 2 to 4 times per day to help trigger a relaxed visual learning state.

In the Visual Learning State, students are typically more attentive and less prone to drift off.

• Visual Reading/Listening

Students can use the Visual Learning State to improve both reading and listening.

When listening to the teacher or professor, practice visualizing the **meaning** of the words, rather than the words, themselves.

When taking notes, instead of taking extensive notes (that frequently miss important points and are more likely to go unread) try making note of only key words and phrases to 'trigger' the visual memory.

When reading, focus on visualizing the meaning of the words rather than the sound of the words.

It may also help to break reading into small 'chunks' by pausing at the end of a paragraph or page for two to three seconds and visualize the content/meaning of what you just read.

When you're finished reading, pause for 30 seconds and visually replay what you just read.

As with listening, write down key words and phrases of your reading to trigger the visual memory.

• Seeing by Touch

Touching and manipulating objects creates a Visual-Spatial 'map' of the experience. Learning by doing is a great strategy for many Visually Dominant students.

• Patterns and Context

Many students naturally organize information by patterns and context rather than characteristics and details.

For these students, providing the big picture or the 'why' is more important than just providing examples and explaining 'how'.

For these same students, simply organizing the information by patterns and applications may facilitate memorization of the information.

• Morning Routine

After a good night's sleep, the most important element in our education wave is a relaxed, non-stressful, non-rushed morning routine.

Try to keep it simple, 5-7 steps. A sample morning routine might look something like this:

1. Wake up
2. Get Dressed (10 minutes)
3. Feed the Dog/Cat/Fish (5 minutes)
4. Eat Breakfast (15 minutes)
5. Sensory Exercises, see Chapter 18 (5 minutes)
6. Spelling/Vocabulary Words (5 minutes)
7. Out the door

Again, Waves—Not Spoons is all about the flow of energy in and out.

To make the most of their educational day, some students may need to take time from lunch and study periods to recharge their 'batteries' with a few minutes of Sensory Exercises.

Even the few minutes between classes can provide the opportunity to do a few minutes of the stress reduction and sensory exercises from Chapters 16 and 17.

• Afterschool/Homework Routine

The next element in our wave is the afterschool/homework routine. Sample elementary school or middle school afterschool/homework routine might look something like this:

1. Arrive home from school
2. Snack: balanced protein/carbs, water—not juice (10 minutes)
3. Play time: exercise, movement--not TV/Video (30-40 minutes)
4. Sensory Exercises (3-5 minutes)
5. Review Old Spelling/Vocabulary (3-5 minutes)
6. New Spelling/Vocabulary (5-10 minutes)
7. Reading (10-15 minutes)
8. Writing (10-15 minutes)
9. Mini-Break: Math Games warm-up (2-3 minutes)
10. Math homework (15-20 minutes)
11. Review New Spelling/Vocabulary (3-5 minutes)
12. Homework MUST be a finite time. No child will last long if his homework takes all afternoon or evening to complete.

I frequently recommend to parents that if an elementary school student requires more than one hour to complete his or her homework, they might want to consider tutoring, an assessment, or other means to address the underlying issues.

The NLC currently offers a free online assessment at **https://swishforfish.com/pages/nlc-sensory-learning-profile**.

• Bedtime Routine

Most grade school children require 8-10 hours of solid sleep. Appropriate bedtimes range from 8:00 to 9:00 pm.

Try to end each day with a simple 5-7 step routine to help facilitate a good night sleep.

Bedtime Routine:

1. Bath time (10 minutes)
2. Pajamas (2 minutes)
3. Brush teeth (3 minutes)
4. Glass of water (2 minutes)
5. Story/reading time (10 minutes)
6. Lights out

It is important that the order of steps do not change. The timing can vary (10-15 minutes story time), but the order should never change.

After a refreshing night sleep, we repeat the process for the education wave to provide a non-rushed, non-stressful morning routine.

Chapter 11: Waves on the Job

Jeremy's day gave us a glimpse of what workdays can look like. The important takeaway is few if any jobs are a constant energy drain all day, every day.

There are almost always opportunities throughout the day to rest and recharge those batteries.

If we look back at our friend Jeremy, can we find a number of flaws with his on the job energy management?

The first thing we saw was that Jeremy had a poor night's sleep.

Without any managing his physical or emotional energy from the prior day, Jeremy had a poor night's sleep and was likely short one or two spoons before he even got out of bed.

We also saw Jeremy sacrifice good nutrition in the interest of time.

Creating energy requires fuel and to have the most energy available, we need to provide the body with reasonably proper nutrition.

While Jeremy received a very temporary energy boost from his carbohydrate and caffeine breakfast, it was very short lived.

Instead of having 10 spoons of energy for the day, it is likely that Jeremy was starting with only 7 or 8.

Because Jeremy's stress tended to bleed over from one activity to another, Jeremy was burning up his emotional spoons simply sitting in a meeting.

Another of Jeremy's serious mistakes was not taking any time during his day to rest and recharge his physical, emotional, or social batteries.

He even sacrificed his lunch hour in a futile attempt to play catch up.

Jeremy held on for the rest of his workday and the drive home. But simply counting spoons was not enough. By the time he arrived home, he had nothing left to give.

Jeremy's Energy Availability in Spoons

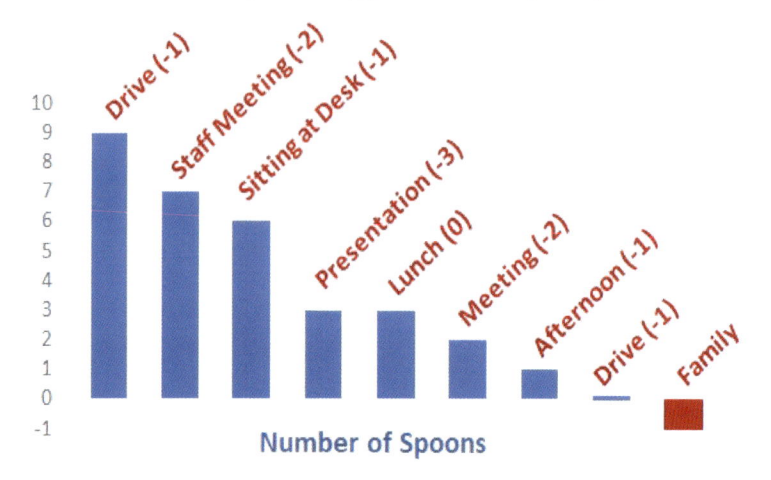

- Drive (-1): 9
- Staff Meeting (-2): 7
- Sitting at Desk (-1): 6
- Presentation (-3): 3
- Lunch (0): 3
- Meeting (-2): 2
- Afternoon (-1): 1
- Drive (-1): 0
- Family: -1

Number of Spoons

Without making any distinction between the drains on his physical energy, emotional energy, and social energy, it all became conflated into one big energy suck.

Had Jeremy used the Waves—Not Spoons Model, he might have had a very different day.

If Jeremy had used a few stress reduction techniques and a basic bedtime routine, he might have had a more refreshing night sleep and begin his day with his energy batteries fully charged (all of his spoons) rather than just some of them.

Instead of hitting the snooze alarm, Jeremy might have taken the time to have a more nutritious breakfast instead of coffee and a bagel, saving him or even adding another spoon.

If Jeremy had left for work just a few minutes earlier, he could have relaxed on the drive to work—possibly listening to refreshing music or inspirational audio book.

At work, Jeremy might also have passed on that glazed doughnut had he not skipped breakfast. He might even have chosen an herbal tea in lieu of the coffee (caffeine) fix.

With a few key communication skills and a bit more confidence in his rapport-building and communication skills, Jeremy might have had a far more relaxing staff meeting.

There's no question, public speaking to groups large or small is a challenge for many people and Jeremy's anxiety is perfectly understandable.

That said, if Jeremy had availed himself of some basic relaxation and public speaking techniques, his presentation might have been considerably less stressful.

It might be said that Jeremy's stress encompassed three presentations. There was the presentation he played over and over in his mind BEFORE the meeting. There was the presentation he gave at the meeting. And there was the presentation he replayed over and over in his mind AFTER the actual meeting.

It's no surprise that by the time Jeremy arrived home he had zero spoons and nothing to give his family.

How many of us have had days like Jeremy?

Let's take a moment to imagine how Jeremy might have felt with the principles of Waves—Not Spoons.

What we see here is that had Jeremy taken advantage of the time between tasks/events he might have had a much easier day as well as the physical and emotional energy to enjoy his evening and spend meaningful time with his family.

Jeremy's Energy Flow in Waves

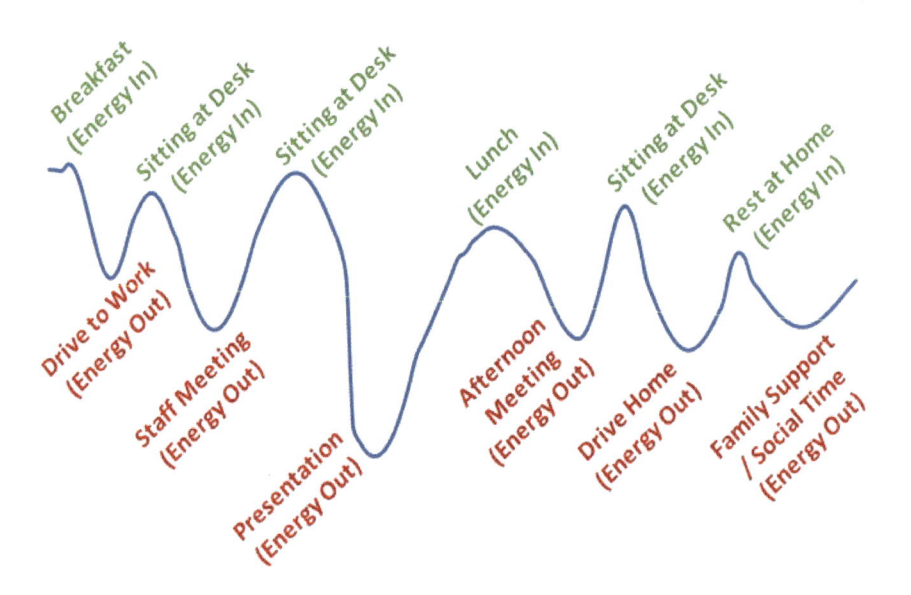

Peaks (Energy In): Breakfast, Sitting at Desk, Sitting at Desk, Lunch, Sitting at Desk, Rest at Home

Troughs (Energy Out): Drive to Work, Staff Meeting, Presentation, Afternoon Meeting, Drive Home, Family Support / Social Time

Remember the quote generally attributed to the white rabbit in Lewis Carrol's Alice in Wonderland, *"The hurrier I go, the behinder I get."*

Take time to recharge those batteries. It is always preferable to structure our days to end with feelings of success and satisfaction regardless of how many spoons we had to work with.

Ending each day with a feeling of success and completeness lends itself to a more restful sleep and increased motivation in the morning.

Chapter 12: Group Event Waves

Group Events can be Home to some and absolute Hell for others.

My guess is, most of us are somewhere in the middle, but if we refer back to our personality profiles in, we can see that feeling comfortable at group events is at least partly the result of our personal strengths and weaknesses.

Those folks who are naturally Dominant Emotional may have an easier time establishing empathy.

Those who are sensory seekers may naturally feel more comfortable in groups and events that are sensory intensive.

Whether conversing with a single person or standing in a group, we can give ourselves a leg up by utilizing our Social and Emotional Energy waves, as well as practicing the Visual Communication techniques outlined in.

As always, establishing empathy and rapport are critical to having a comfortable and fulfilling time at most group events.

If you're in a small group discussion, observe the group dynamics. Perhaps an individual feels the need to be the center of attention.

This is where those questions can really come in handy. You can even interrupt a monologue with a relevant question without seeming rude.

Observe your own Emotional Energy Waves and take the time you need to recharge those batteries.

If needs be, arrive late and leave early. Sneak away in the middle of an event for some sensory processing and stress reduction exercises.

The point is, do what you need to do to stay as relaxed and focused as possible.

Don't be afraid to help the conversation along. Use those relevant questions to expand the discussion by calling on different people.

Be inclusive. If you notice someone seems left out of the discussion, take a question and direct it to that person.

They can always choose not to answer but you might be giving them the permission they need to jump in or just feel included.

And feel free to stretch a bit. The Waves—Not Spoons model will not leave you hanging.

With Spoon Theory, when you've used up all your spoons, you're done. It's time to hide or go home.

But with Waves—Not Spoons, you can manage your emotional energy and if needs be, you can slip away and recharge your emotional batteries with any one of dozens of stress reduction and sensory processing techniques from chapters 16 and 17.

Chapter 13: Public Speaking Waves

There is little question that for most people, public speaking is one of the most challenging social endeavors.

With respect to Waves, public speaking is likely a high-energy event. In many cases, public speaking will require energy usage both in the preparation and delivery of the speaking.

The first step in public speaking waves is too begin in a relaxed focused state. And now we're starting with the maximum physical, emotional, and social energy available.

Ideally, we want to schedule our day around the speaking event. If possible, avoid other major energy needs that day and leave time for a rest and recharge wave immediately before and after the speaking event if possible.

Next, we want to be as prepared as possible for our speaking engagement.

If time allows, rehearse the speech several times while visualizing a very receptive audience.

This is the time to address your nervousness—BEFORE you speak.

If we're delivering a prepared speech, try to keep the speech to 3 or 4 main points if possible. Be familiar with the content of the speech and be prepared to answer questions about the content of your speech.

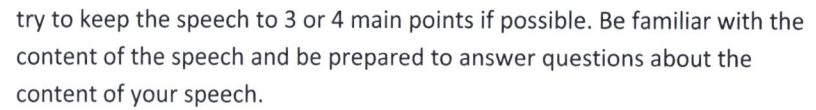

There have been many books written about public speaking and specifically about the fear of public speaking.

Unfortunately, most of them fail to grasp the basic underlying source of the fear, that being a lack of rapport. It's the same with our personal relationships and other events, the source of fear is a lack of rapport.

When we're in rapport, everyone feels more comfortable. Those we're with can feel more comfortable because there's a neurological connection that allows everyone to let their guard down.

When we're in rapport, we don't have to GUESS where we stand or if our message is understood, because we KNOW where we stand, and we KNOW our message is understood.

We've discussed how to create rapport at home at school at work. But how do we create rapport with a group of people?

As with our other interactions in relationships, the first step in creating rapport is to be relaxed. When we are relaxed, the noise in our heads subsides and we have a far better change of reading the people around us.

Creating rapport is all about putting your audience at ease. We included a list of strategies for creating rapport in Chapter 8: Communication Waves, but when speaking to a group, the easiest way to create rapport is to tailor your message to the likes and needs of your audience.

Another powerful rapport-building strategy is to tell a personal story that allows the audience to identify themselves and their struggles in you.

To help hold your audience's attention, begin your story, telling only the first 80% or so. Then deliver your content. Finish up by telling the conclusion of your story.

The old rule of speaking, tell them what you're going to tell them, then tell them, then tell them what you told them still holds true as a model for speaking and writing:

- thesis/introduction
- body/information
- summary/conclusion

Again, there are many books on public speaking techniques.

In addition to the stress reduction exercises in Chapter 17: Emotional Energy Refresh Techniques, there are additional resources listed in Appendix A: Additional Resources.

Chapter 14: Project Management Waves

Adding waves to our project management can help us dramatically improve our success professionally and personally.

It is important that each person understand their own energy flow.

Marathoners may find it advantageous to power though entire projects or large tasks and rest/recharge when the job is done.

Others (Sprinters) may function more effectively by first breaking down projects and large tasks into smaller subtasks, taking shorter breaks to rest/recharge between each subtask.

Project Waves

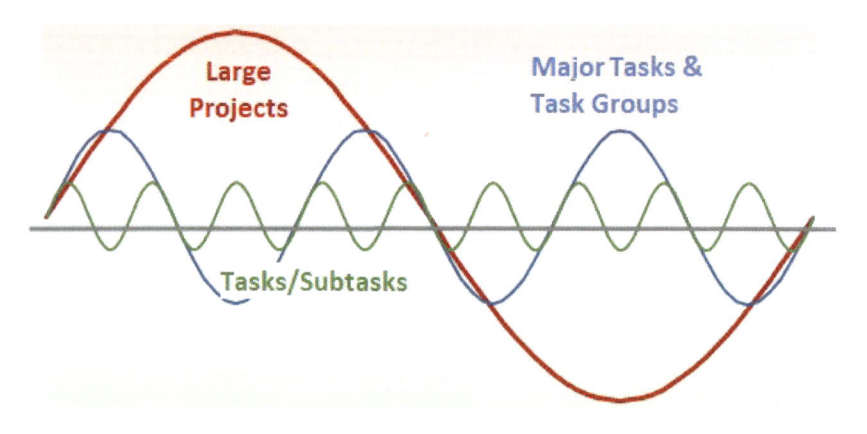

Large Projects — Major Tasks & Task Groups — Tasks/Subtasks

Neither approach is right or wrong. What's important is finding the wave that's right for you and making the necessary adjustments.

Many folks will find that a simple top-down approach to organizing projects is right for them.

Others may find that a mind-mapping or flow-chart works for them.

Either is ok. The following diagrams illustrate two simple models for breaking projects into tasks and subtasks.

Top-down Project Breakdown

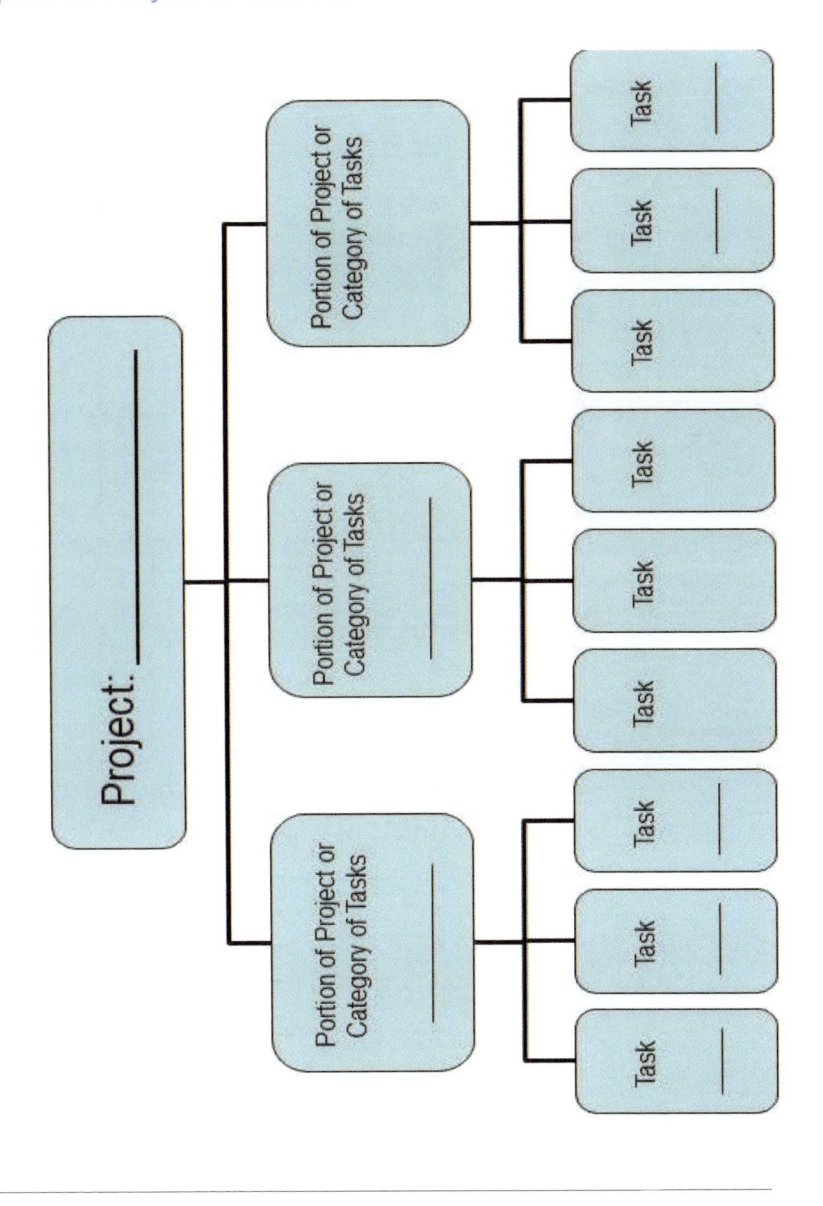

Flow-Chart/Mind-Map

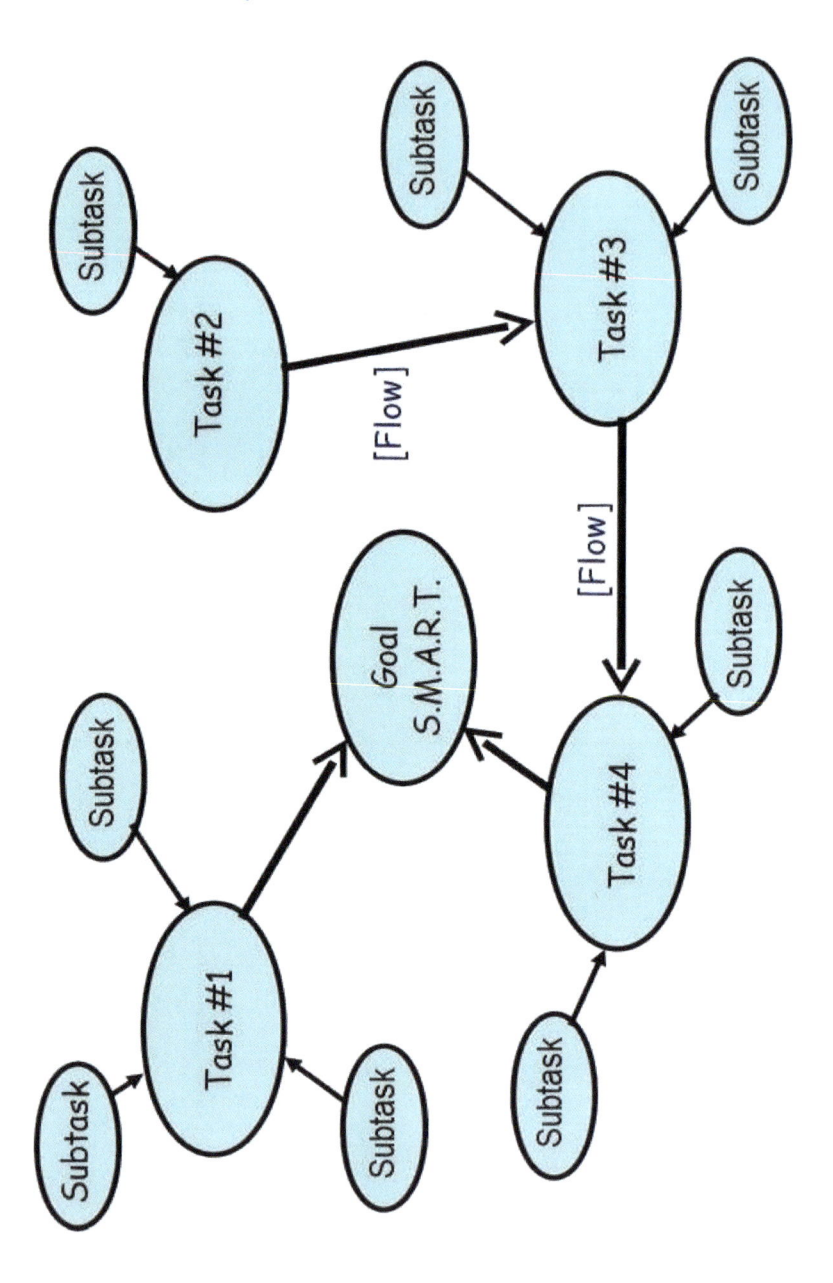

What we're saying is trust your gut (feelings). Select an organizational strategy that is right for you.

If you find yourself resisting the project/task or the project/task feels overwhelming, it might be worth further examining that project/task.

One way for a person to gauge which approach might be best is to simply imagine the task and see how it feels.

• Procrastination

A word on procrastination. If you find yourself procrastinating, consider asking yourself these three questions:

Do I have the ability and resources to complete this?

Do I have enough time to do this?

Is this important to me and my goals?

If the answer to questions 1 or 2 is, "No", it is important to resolve the conflict. Break the project down into pieces and ask questions 1 and 2 again. Repeat as needed until the answer is, "Yes" for all parts of the assignment.

If the answer to question 3 is, "No", it is important to review the outcome of the project and compare it to YOUR goals. If they are not connected, it may be prudent to review the project against your values or against completing goals.

Again, trust your feelings. Trust your gut.

• Demand Avoidance

In addition to procrastination, some persons may avoid accepting some tasks due to a phenomenon called, Demand Avoidance.

Demand Avoidance typically manifests as a reluctance to accept commitment and/or responsibility. It is sometimes the reaction to chronic and repeated failure or criticism, especially during childhood.

Demand Avoidance is typically the result of repeated negative experiences growing up.

To overcome Demand Avoidance, those past experiences must be addressed.

Chapter 15: Goal Setting

In applying the Waves model to goal setting, we can strive to make the most of your available energy by eliminating activities that are not aligned with our values and goals.

One popular model for goal setting is to strive for SMART Goals. SMART Goals are: Specific, Measurable, Attainable, Realistic, and Timed.

Specific – No generalizations. "I will be a writer," is not specific. "I will write a book about relationships," is specific.

Measurable – The goal should be quantifiable. "I will be rich," is not measurable. "I will have $100,000 in my savings account," is measurable.

Attainable – The goal should be attainable (in the real world). "I will own Hawaii", is probably not attainable. "I will own a 120 foot Yacht," is probably attainable.

Realistic – The goal should be realistic for the individual. "I will own a 120 foot Yacht," is probably attainable if my plan involves becoming the CEO of a Major company. But if my life plan is to become a teacher or police officer, owning a 120 foot Yacht is probably not realistic.

Timed – All achievements exist in time. Valid goals must have a time limit. "I want to go fishing someday," is a wish— not a goal. "I'm going fishing next Tuesday," is a goal.

To avoid frustration, a sense of failure, and possible burnout, it is critical that we time our goals to allow for periods of rest and recharge.

One way to test our goals and avoid unpleasant surprises is to review our current and set new ones at least once a week.

This weekly review is a good time to test your goals for emotional resistance or lack of commitment.

If a goal feels overwhelming or does not feel right, we may need to ask the three procrastination questions. We should take a few minutes in the evening to review the progress we made on our goals for the day, make adjustments if needed, and review our goals for the next day.

Surprises and sudden plot twists are great for movies but *not* for projects and goals. Weekly and daily reviews or our goals help prevent or limit surprises. They also help us make the necessary adjustments when needed.

• SMART Goal Visualization

1. Select a time when you can sit comfortably and will not be disturbed for 5-10 minutes.
2. Close your eyes and imagine yourself floating.
3. Imagine your life as a series of waves extending from the present, back into the past and out into your future.
4. Visualize one of your SMART Goals.
5. Visualize the goal as the end result—the point at which you can look back on and know you have achieved your goal.
6. Allow yourself to feel strong feelings of success, accomplishment, pride and contribution as you picture achievement of your goal.
7. Intensify your goal by breathing three strong breaths into the image of your goal. See it grow bigger, brighter, and stronger.
8. Take your goal and float it up and out into your future to the point in time at which you see yourself completing your goal.
9. Remember, the timing of your goals should allow for periods of rest and recharge.
10. Drop your goal into your future. Hear it lock into place.
11. Turn around facing the past and return to the present.
12. Repeat the above steps for each goal on your list. Add, remove, and replace goals as needed.

Remember to *always* trust your feelings and your gut.

This does not mean to abandon a goal because of resistance or reluctance.

It does mean to *not* ignore the feelings and instincts. It means to re-examine that goal with those three procrastination questions.

As always, please make use of whatever resources are available, including those listed on our web site and in Appendix B: Resources.

Chapter 16: Physical Energy Exercises

The very first rule of managing our physical energy is to understand how we process different types of energy and to respect our limitations.

High & Low Energy Waves

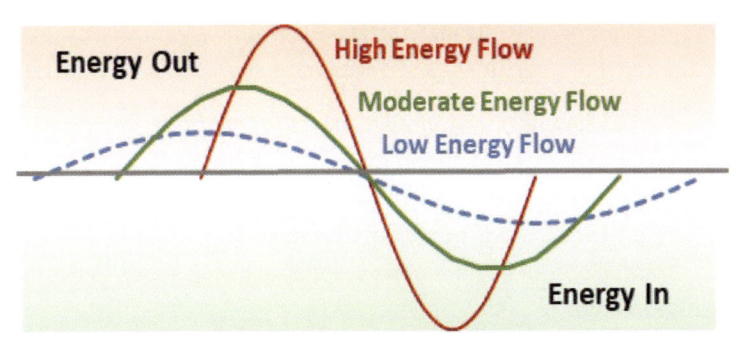

Energy Out — High Energy Flow — Moderate Energy Flow — Low Energy Flow — Energy In

While this advice may seem contrary to that of every Life Coach on the planet, it is nonetheless critical to understand and respect our physical, emotional and social limitations.

This understanding provides us with a framework within which we can exercise our strategies.

As we become more confident and secure in our activities, we open up new opportunities and new possibilities.

The techniques described in this text is not an exhaustive list. They are only examples of techniques and strategies that people can implement throughout their day to replenish physical energy expended in their daily activities.

To be clear, we are NOT addressing any possible medical issues and nothing in this book should be construed as a replacement for counseling, therapy, or sound Medical advice.

There are all kinds of activities that can cause us to feel tired, fatigued, and other forms of energy drain.

• Breathing Energy Refresh

The goal of this exercise is to refresh our body and mind by oxygenating the blood.

As part of this exercise, we want to shift our breathing from shallow and high in the chest to slow, deep, and down in the belly.

1. Start by finding a comfortable place to stand or sit.
2. Take a slow deep breath in for a count of eight seconds pushing down on the diaphragm.
3. Hold the breath for a count of four seconds.
4. Breathe out for a count of six seconds allowing your shoulders to relax and drop.
5. Repeat this deep breathing four times.
6. As you breathe in and out, focus on your breathing. Imagine breathing in all that oxygen and breathing out carbon dioxide.

For the first few times this exercise may feel like a stretch. That's okay. Many of us get used to more shallow breathing high in the chest. This is a chance to really fill those lungs and oxygenate the blood.

• Get the Blood Flowing

Sitting or standing for long periods can leave the body feeling stiff and fatigued.

While our first instinct may be to play catch-up by skipping breaks and working through lunches (keeping your nose to the grindstone), this strategy may actually be counterproductive.

Like our friend, Jeremy, we'll simply run out of energy before the end of the day.

Instead of trying to 'power through' breaks and lunches, try standing up and walking away from your desk/work for 10-15 minutes once or twice a day.

• Water, Water, Everywhere

It may or may not come as a surprise that many Americans spend much of their lives chronically dehydrated.

Many Americans have replaced clean, clear water with soft drinks and juice. Others consume coffee (a natural diuretic). And still others live on energy drinks high in caffeine.

Chronic dehydration can cause a variety of symptoms, including fatigue and lack of concentration. Simply including eight 16-ounce glasses of clean, clear water in your daily activities can provide a real energy boost and even improve focus and attention.

If plain water isn't your 'cup of tea', try adding a few drops of lemon juice or other natural flavoring, but try to avoid sugar and artificial sweeteners.

• Eat Healthy and Often

Like many busy folks, our friend, Jeremy, was trying to live on caffeine and fast-burning carbohydrates. And like those other busy folks, Jeremy's energy slowly and steadily declined until, by the end of the day, he had nothing left to give.

Frequent meals and snacks (every 90 to 120 minutes) is a healthy rhythm and can keep the body from going into starvation mode.

In lieu of caffeine and simple carbohydrates (simple sugars, white flour, etc.), try to go with a combination of complex carbohydrates (whole grains, peas, beans, and vegetables) and protein (seeds and nuts, beans, legumes, lean meats, poultry, fish, eggs, and cheese).

Try to limit milk due to high sugar content and soy products due to phytoestrogens.

• Physical Exercise

It goes without saying that regular physical exercise is critical to physical health.

What is lesser known is that the specific type exercise and the intensity of the exercise are far less important than simply getting some physical exercise on the daily basis.

For many people, just 12-18 minutes of low impact, low intensity exercise every day can make world of difference.

If appropriate to your health and physical ability, at least 3 times a week, try to get your heart rate up to 60% of its maximum (varies with age) for 15-20 minutes.

This can be a brisk walk outside, time on the treadmill, circuit training, hot yoga, dancing! Anything that will get the heart pumping and the blood flowing. A few types of beneficial exercise include:

- Walking
- Jogging
- Swimming
- Dancing
- Yoga
- Tai Chi
- Weightlifting

Again, the important thing is to try to make exercise part of your daily routine.

As always, don't engage in any new diet or exercise without consulting your physician.

• Guided Imagery

The NLC has a number of guided imagery tracks (see Eye of the Storm) available that can help refresh the mind and the body. These tracks are especially powerful as the voice overlays are available with binaural beats and positive subliminal messaging.

Remember to know your ways. What has been addressed so far are merely sample techniques and strategies that are available to help refresh and recharge those physical batteries.

The key is to know your own Waves and how best to schedule these tools into your daily and weekly activities.

• Massage

For some people, getting a massage is a luxury—for others, it is a necessity.

Massages can help relieve emotional stress as well as physical tension.

• Acupuncture

Acupuncture and acupressure have long been used to help alleviate a variety of ailments and symptoms, including pain relief.

The effectiveness seems to vary widely from person to person.

- Biofeedback

Biofeedback has proven helpful to some people in reducing stress and chronic pain.

Biofeedback typically requires use of a specialized machine (and an operator) to administer the biofeedback sessions. The effects of a session may be hours or days depending on the individual and issue being treated.

The biggest drawbacks of biofeedback are cost ($50-$100 per 1-hr treatment) and lack of permanence.

Some issues may require one or two treatments per week for months, years or indefinitely to continue receiving the benefits.

Chapter 17: Emotional Energy Refresh

Emotional energy refresh techniques are included only as examples of techniques and strategies that people can implement throughout their day to replenish physical, emotional, and social energy expended in their daily activities.

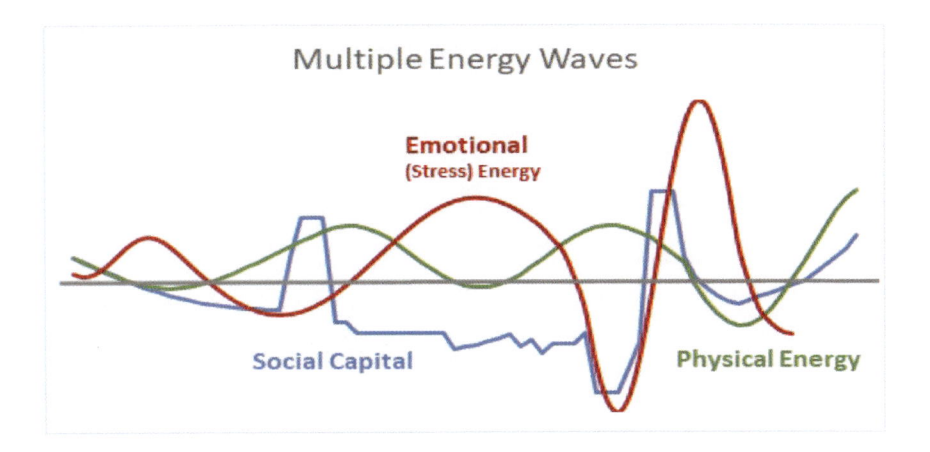

Multiple Energy Waves

Emotional (Stress) Energy

Social Capital   Physical Energy

These exercises are only temporary measures. The intention is to take advantage of those times during our day when we can 'recharge' our physical, emotional, or social batteries.

We are *not* addressing the underlying causes of emotional issues with these exercises and again, nothing in this book should be construed as a replacement for counseling, therapy, or sound medical advice.

• Expanded Awareness; Relax and Focus

1. Start by finding a comfortable place to sit where you will not be disturbed for a few minutes.
2. Find a spot on the wall at least a few feet away and a few feet above eye level.
3. Breathe slow and deep as you keep your eyes on that spot.
4. As you focus on the spot, continue to breathe deep in the belly, letting all your muscles relax.
5. Now, allow yourself to become aware of everything around you.
6. Without moving your eyes from the spot, expand your awareness all the way out to your peripheral vision.
7. Notice you can be aware of everything happening around you without moving your eyes from the spot.
8. Maintain this focused awareness for one minute while continuing deep, relaxed breathing.

• Power Nap

Don't underestimate the power of a short nap during the day! A short, 15-20 minute nap can clear the head and refresh thinking.

A word of caution on naps. Don't go over 20 minutes. If you enter a full 90-minute sleep cycle and interrupt in the middle, you could wake up groggy and disoriented instead of refreshed and alert.

• Quick Disconnect

The purpose of this simple exercise is to quickly 'detach' or dissociate from sudden and potentially overwhelming emotions.

The entire exercise is to stop, look up. Look up towards the ceiling.

If you wish, you can count backwards from four to one while breathing slowly and deeply.

This simple exercise can help us avoid an emotional response that may not be useful or appropriate to the current situation.

You can test this technique when you're engaged in a nervous tic or other behavior (rocking, leg bounce, twisting hair, etc.) and observing if the nervous behavior stops within seconds of looking up.

See Appendix A: Additional Resources for links to videos and other resources.

• Juggling to Relax and Focus

Because of its profound effect on the nervous system, juggling is one of the *best* stress reduction and focusing exercises I've ever come across.

Yes, juggling has a bit of a learning curve, but the basic inside juggle is not as difficult and you might think.

In addition to the instructions below, there are a number of YouTube videos, including our own, that make learning to juggle quick and easy.

Step One: Hot Potato

Standing in place with arms bent and elbows at your side, gently toss a juggling ball (provided with this program) from hand to hand with a rhythm of about one or two tosses per second.

Try to imagine a spot about a foot above your head. Now, toss the ball to that spot.

Practice 5-10 minutes a day.

Step Two: Double Hot Potato.

When Hot Potato becomes relatively easy, take one juggling ball in each hand, alternating with each hand, gently toss the balls in the air to that imaginary spot above your head and catch with the opposite hand.

Alternate tossing left and right, respectively. Work up to a pace of two tosses (one with each hand) per second. Focus on tossing the balls almost straight up with a steady rhythm. Toss, toss… catch, catch.

At this point, don't put too much emphasis on catching the balls. Focus on the rhythm of the toss and the point in space.

Step Three: Toss, Toss, Toss

As this exercise becomes relatively easy, the final step is to add a third ball. Decide which hand is more comfortable to start tossing with, and always start with two balls in that hand.

Place one ball between the thumb and first two fingers. Place a second ball between the palm and the three remaining fingers. Begin by tossing the first ball, then, the ball in the opposite hand and finally the third ball from the palm of the first hand.

Toss each ball only once—toss, toss, toss.

You'll notice at the end of the toss, toss, toss, the two balls are now in the opposite hand. Move the third ball back to your dominant hand and repeat—toss, toss, toss. At this point, resist the urge to keep juggling.

Spend some time, practicing toss, toss, toss, until both tossing and catching feels natural.

Step Four: Juggling

The final step is to just keep going. Maybe try four tosses, then five, six, and so on.

For added stress relief, build up to juggling while counting backwards or reciting the alphabet. My favorite stress reduction exercise is juggling while reciting PI (3.14159265358979...)

As with most of the other exercises, breathe deep and slow, relax the neck and shoulders, keep your focus on the exercise.

- **Thumb Juggling**

A simpler, easier alternative to learning to juggle is the "Juggling Made Easy" app available <u>free</u> for both iPhone and Android devices.

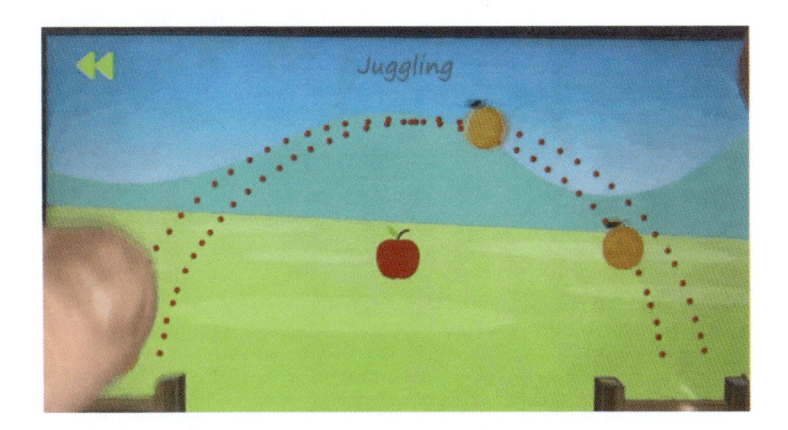

By engaging both thumbs and eyes in a simple, repetitive, non-linear movement, this easy-to-use app helps shift the Autonomic Nervous System (ANS) into a more relaxed and focused state.

Originally developed for clients at the Neuro-linguistic Learning Center, this exercise is also included in our "Relax and Focus" app.

See Appendix A: Additional Resources *for links to videos and other resources.*

• Relax and Focus App

The "Relax and Focus" app is available free for both iPhone and Android devices.

This easy-to-use app takes just 2 minutes to help a person feel more relaxed and focused.

It works by interrupting the normal neurological stress response enabling the person to assume a more relaxed posture.

Originally developed for clients at the Neuro-linguistic Learning Center, most users find that just two minutes, twice a day, can make a world of difference, especially when combined with a comprehensive sensory processing and stress reduction program.

• Eye of the Storm

The news was clear. The storm was coming. Martin was just nailing down boards over the last windows on his home. He could hear the winds increasing. The family car and a 6500Watt generator were safely stored in the garage along with 20 gallons of gasoline and 40 one-gallon water bottles. The pantry was well-stocked with batteries, toilet paper, and non-perishable foods. There was little to do but wait.

As the storm grew louder rain, hail, leaves, branches, paper and other debris filled the air. Martin secured his home's front and back doors and double-checked the flashlights.

Within a few hours the storm had reached peak intensity. Even from inside the house, the sound was frightening.

It wasn't long before the lights flickered and then went out. Martin turned on a flashlight and peeked outside.

It had grown darker. The wind was taking anything not fastened down—large branches, toys, papers, and now shingles, shutters.

The rain and hail were coming down in sheets, swirling with all the other debris and litter kicked up by the storm.

It was complete chaos. It was as if his entire world was dragged into a swirl of wind and rain. It seemed like an eternity had passed and the storm was still raging.

But as Martin watched and listened, he could feel a shift in the intensity of the storm. It seemed to weaken and then, suddenly, everything went quiet.

Absolutely silent...no wind...no sound...nothing.

Martin realized that he had entered the eye of the storm—that place where everything becomes completely quiet. The stillness was so profound, so inviting, that even Martin's own thoughts and feelings seemed to disappear.

It is only human for each of us to experience some amount of chaos in our lives.

Events, relationships, and social dynamics can feel overwhelming. In addition, our own thoughts, feelings, and sensory perceptions all intertwine in a complex, ever-changing dynamic.

This dynamic could easily be described as chaotic. We might even imagine the chaos of Martin's hurricane as analogy to the chaos in our lives.

It begs the question can we, like Martin, step away from the chaos, and experience that quiet and calm at the eye of the storm?

- Stepping into the eye of the storm

Stand in the middle of the room at a time when you will not be disturbed for at least 10 minutes.

Imagine you are standing in the midst of the hurricane that is your life. This hurricane contains your family, friends, work, your feelings and emotions, all the pieces of your life are caught up in swirling chaos.

Feel the storm's intensity and complexity— its chaos. Notice your own thoughts and feelings. Notice that your conscious mind may be completely overwhelmed by the experience. You may feel confusion, frustration, or even fear at your inability to process the complex information that makes up your 'storm'.

As you stand inside of the storm, feeling its power, be aware that just right behind you is the eye of the storm.

Inside the eye there is complete serenity and silence —no thoughts, no feelings, nothing except awareness of the storm beyond.

And imagine that this stillness, this quiet, is only one step behind you. Taking one step back would take you out of the storm and into the quiet calm at the eye of the storm.

Slowly countdown from three to one. On the count of one, take one step back out of the storm and into the eye.

Three - feel the full intensity of the storm—everything going on around you—total chaos.

Two – everything going on around you and even your own thoughts and feelings, all part of the storm.

One – take one step back, out of the storm and into the eye... out of the chaos in into the calm stillness.

Deep breath in and out, feel the calm, the stillness, the silence.

Notice that you can still see the storm. It's just there in front of you in all its fury, but it's not you.

You are the witness, the observer. You can see the storm, including your own thoughts and feelings. You are no longer the storm.

The storm is the storm and you are you.

Stand in the eye of the storm for one minute. Breathing in and out, slowly and deeply.

Visualize the storm, the chaos going on all around you, but not in you. It's all out there—the good, the bad, the indifferent.

After a minute or so, when ready, count forward from one to three and step back into the storm. Again, feel the force of the storm, the intensity, the thoughts and emotions.

We're not going to stay in the storm.

After 10 to 15 seconds in the storm, count back from three to one and return into the eye of the storm. Again, feel the serenity. Once again, the storm is out there.

Take a few deep breaths then, feeling the stillness and silence, count forwards from one to three and return into the storm for a few seconds.

After 10 to 15 seconds in the storm, count back one more time from three to one and step back into the eye of the storm feeling the stillness, the silence.

Now, take that internal stillness and go on with your day.

_____

Note: For best results practice this exercise a few times when you're not overly stressed or overwhelmed.

By building your experience stepping out of the storm and into the eye, you'll be able to release more stress *and* handle situations that may once have overwhelmed you.

• A Glass of Wine

For many persons a glass of wine with dinner can help reduce stress and improve digestion.

Again, this is ONE glass of wine per day for some people. Obviously, those persons with a history of alcohol or drug abuse should probably not indulge in the consumption of alcohol.

Chapter 18: Sensory Techniques

In this chapter, we outline some of our best sensory techniques. These techniques can help reduce feelings of stress, anxiety, anger, and fear by redirecting the flow of sensory information.

The exact neurological effect created by these exercises is some form of <u>bilateral hemispheric integration</u>. That is, the two hemispheres of the brain working together in some coordinated fashion.

This is possible because each hemisphere of the brain controls (and receives feedback from one side of the body. So, when, for example, we touch the right hand to the left knee, the two hemispheres of the brain must coordinate (integrate) their respective activities.

These techniques are designed to evoke specific neurological responses and typically take just one or two minutes.

If these exercises are new to your, try the simpler exercises first and gradually work up to the more advanced exercises (like juggling).

Most of these exercises are easily incorporated into a person's daily routine.

And many of these exercises can be completed quietly and discreetly--on the job or in public - without drawing any attention to one's self.

• Sensory Doodle

If you find yourself stressing out at a meeting, try this inconspicuous stress reduction doodle.

Using a pencil, pen, or your finger, trace the figure-8 or infinity sign (sideways figure-8) on your paper, desk or even your leg under the table.

Trace the figure Ten times in one direction and then ten times in the opposite direction.

Again, the focus is on the diagonal lines. Why? Because it takes both hemispheres of the brain to draw a diagonal line.

• Sensory Eyes

This exercise is another bilateral hemispheric integration.

Imagine an infinity sign (or sideways 8), approximately shoulder width slightly above eye level.

Trace the infinity sign ten (10) times. Then, reverse direction and trace ten (10) more times.

Note: If you're an adult working with a child, you can hold your index finger 18"-24" away from the child's face, slightly above eye level and create the infinity sign motion for the child to follow.

This exercise is included in several NLC free apps including, "Reading with Dyslexia," "Spelling Made Easy," and "Relax and Focus."

• Sensory Hook up

Standing straight and relaxed, cross one foot over the other so your left foot is on the right and your right foot in on the left, heels flat on the floor. With arms out in front of you, put the backs of your hands together.

Next move the left hand up and over your right hand then down so your right hand in on the left and your left hand is on the right palms together. Clasp your fingers.

Next, bring your clasped hands down under your chin (keep your balance).

Once your tangled up, look up and pick a spot on the ceiling. With just your eyes (keeping your head still), trace an infinity sign with the crossing point at that spot.

Draw the infinity sign (or sideways figure-8) 10 times one direction and then 10 times the opposite direction.

• Sensory Walking

The first exercise is a simple bilateral hemispheric integration. We start by walking forwards then backwards. We'll count out loud from 1 to 10 going forwards and then counting back down from 10 to 1 when walking backwards.

While walking, we're going to touch the palm of our hand to our *opposite* knee with each step.

(Note for young children and first timers: you might practice this exercise while marching in place and add in the forwards and back later.)

Next, we're going to add focus and attention.

Find a spot above eye level off to your left, maybe where the walls and the ceiling come together, and stay focused on that spot while you do your cross-walk exercise.

Our goal is 10 steps forward and 10 steps back. Repeat 4-5 times each.

Have good posture, but not stiff.

Keep your shoulders and neck relaxed.

You chin should be slightly raised above horizontal.

Breath slow and deep, pushing the belly out with each breath in.

One option for this exercise is to have the supervising adult walk in front of the child for the child to 'mirror'. This allows the adult to set a slow, steady pace for the exercise.

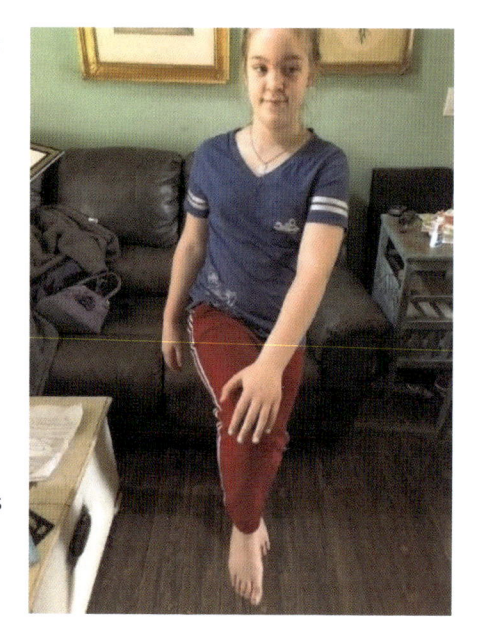

• Finger-Knitting

This is a simple exercise that most children can learn to do at an early age.

The basic exercise is to take a length of heavy yarn and begin with a slip knot.

Then pull the 'long' side of the yard through the loop of the slip knot to create a new knot.

Pull the yarn on one side of the new loop to close/tighten up the first loop.

Repeat by pulling the 'long' side of the yard through the loop to create the next knot /loop.

Continue making new knot/loops for as long as you like.

This is a great exercise for travel, seminars, and any other time when you're forced to sit for long periods of time.

• Finger-Weaving

Similar to finger-knitting, finger weaving uses the four fingers on one hand to act as the loom.

Begin with a slip-knot around the index finger and weave the yarn back and forth around the other fingers to start the weave.

Wrap the long end of the yarn straight across the top.

One by one loop the yard around each finger over the straight piece and over the end of the finger.

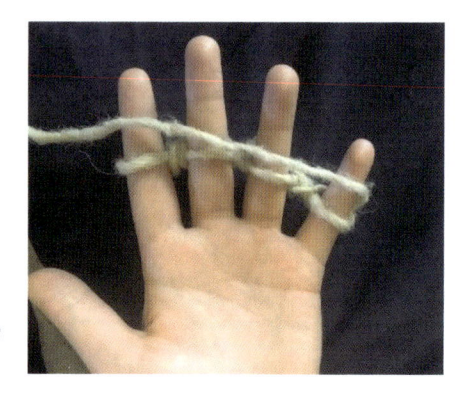

After all finger weaves are looped to the back, lay the free end back over the top of the hand.

After a few minutes, turn your hand over and there should be the beginning of a net.

Continue the pattern for 5-10 minutes.

In addition to the bilateral hemispheric integration and reducing stress, this exercise can help improve fine motor skills.

- **Stimming**

While this is merely a sample of Sensory Exercises, it would be remiss to not include a word on "stimming".

Stimming (or stims, as they are sometimes called) are frequently referenced in psychology as behaviors (or symptoms) commonly displayed by many autistic persons.

Beyond mere behaviors, stims can have a profound effect on a person's physiological and neurological state.

Pacing, swinging, rocking and spinning, can help reduce stress and improve focus and attention by placing the person's orientation in constant motion. This motion helps shift the Autonomic Nervous System from fight or flight to a more relaxed state.

Leg bouncing, finger drumming, foot jiggling, pencil tapping, hand flapping, can help release nervous energy.

Other stims, like singing, whistling or humming can help reduce stress and increase focus by replacing random (intrusive) thoughts with simple, familiar words, thoughts and rhythmic patterns.

Another benefit of making constant noise is it fills in the silent gaps between random, unexpected, and intrusive noises. They can also provide a context of familiarity, like whistling in the dark.

Repetitive blinking creates something akin to a strobe effects, breaking visual perception up into discrete images or frames. It also helps direct focus and attention away from the auditory and to the visual.

Other nervous habits that provide some sensory stimulation and mental distraction include fingernail biting, hair twirling, and knuckle cracking.

Chapter 19: Establishing Rapport

The fact is we are neurologically 'wired' to like people who are like us, especially those in our family or community/tribe. So, establishing a sense of relatedness goes a long way towards establishing rapport.

The first step in establishing rapport is to find common ground with the person or persons with whom you're communicating.

Establishing rapport can be as simple as sharing things you have in common, such as place of birth, the college you both attended or your favorite sports team.

Rapport can also be established unconsciously by triggering the other person's parasympathetic nervous system.

While this may sound like science fiction, it is a well-established by empirical evidence and have long been used in therapy, sales, and a variety of other careers and professions.

These techniques can be as overt as matching another person's posture, gestures, and facial expressions, or as subtle as matching their breathing, heart rate, and emotional state.

The amazing thing is that these techniques can work fairly quickly—some in a few minutes, others as little as a few seconds.

The third path to establishing rapport is by association. When people hear or see you being accepted by others who are like themselves, they will often perceive a sense of relatedness with little or no personal confirmation.

This community of relatedness is sometimes referred to as a person's sphere of influence.

• Match & Mirror: Posture

Matching posture is probably the simplest and easiest non-verbal communication that helps establish an unconscious feeling of rapport.

The basic technique is to simply copy a natural approximation of the other person's posture. For example, if they are standing straight and stiff, you stand relatively straight and stiff. If they are standing (or sitting) slouched, you stand/sit relatively slouched.

A word on seating positions. When possible, try to avoid sitting directly across the table from the other person. Instead, sit next to or off to the left or right side. This has a number of effects including not having the stare into the other person's eyes all evening.

• Match & Mirror: Gestures

Matching gestures can be tricky. It's important to keep your actions as subtle and as inconspicuous as possible. The last thing we want is for the other person to become consciously aware of our motions or worse, to feel like we're mocking or making fun of him.

That said, if they lean forward (like they are very interested), you may lean forward. If they lean back, you lean back. But if they lean to the left, you might lean towards the right. If they look up and to the left, you look up and to the right. Get the idea?

If you're sitting down to dinner, notice their rhythm for eating. If they pick up their glass to take a drink, you pick up your glass. If they take a bite of food, you take a bit of food.

You can also cross-match or mirror. If he takes a drink, you take a bite. If he picks up his napkin, you pick up your spoon.

We *must* assure emphasize that these motions appear *natural* and *never* forced.

The real gift comes when you've practiced matching and mirroring until they become automatic and unconscious behaviors. You're still in control, but you can do them without thinking.

• Match & Mirror: Breathing

Matching and mirroring another person's breathing is absolutely one of the most powerful rapport-building techniques. It can be done anytime and anywhere.

Breathing is natural and omni-present. For all practical purposes, matching a person's breathing puts your entire physiology in sync.

The basic technique is to match the rhythm of other person's breathing. If he is breathing fast and shallow, you breathe fast and shallow. If he is breathing slow and deep, you breathe slow and deep. It's that simple.

Now, you can also mirror a person's breathing with almost any other motion or part of the body.

With many of my students, I would mirror their breathing by slightly nodding my head. This gave me the ability to talk in my rhythm while continuing to match the rhythm of their breathing.

Psychologist Milton Ericson was a quadriplegic who was confined to a wheelchair. He would create unconscious rapport with his clients through the use of specific language patterns and by matching his client's breathing with his index finger.

• Matching Language Patterns

Matching language patterns is not quite as simple as matching and mirroring physiology, but it does have the benefit of encouraging and supporting active listening.

The technique is *not* to match everything the speaker says. That would be ridiculous and likely elicit the phrase, "Don't Copy me."

Instead, we want to listen for specific words and phrases that indicate how the speaker is perceiving and processing Sensory information.

Sensory Perception Words/Phrases

Visual-Spatial
I can *imagine*...
Can you *see/picture*...
It's *clear* to me.
bright/vivid

Auditory
I *hear/heard* you
loud and clear
Sounds good to me
That *rings* true.

Sensory Processing Words/Phrases

Logic/Reason
Makes sense to me
Sounds *right/logical*
Think about it
reasonable/rational

Feeling/Emotion
It *feels* like...
appreciate
passionate
loving/caring

Most people will tend to use one group of perception words and one group of processing words. Once you see/hear the dominant pattern, you can match the person's pattern rather than repeating back their exact words.

Chapter 20: Brain Waves

Brain entrainment is a fascinating and useful phenomenon.

In its simplest form, it utilizes a technology called binaural beats wherein different auditory frequencies are sent to the left and right ears and, thereby to the left and right hemispheres of the brain.

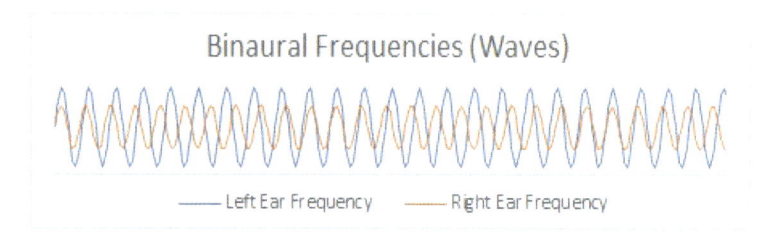

Binaural Frequencies (Waves)

— Left Ear Frequency   — Right Ear Frequency

The two hemispheres of the brain then combine these two separate frequencies to create a third frequency.

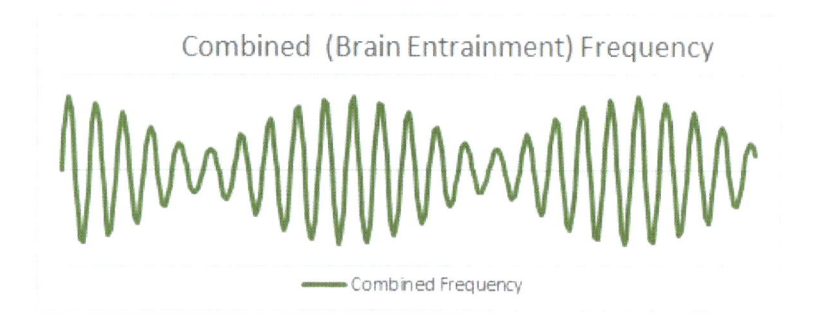

Combined (Brain Entrainment) Frequency

— Combined Frequency

It is this third frequency to which the brain synchronizes itself. This synchronization has some amazing side effects.

Extensive research has shown that different frequencies can dramatically affect the brain and how it processes information.

More importantly, these frequencies can dramatically affect how we think and feel.

There are brain entrainment frequencies to improve focus and attention, relaxation, creativity, excitement and even sleep.

NLC can provide individualized Brain Entrainment and Subliminal Motivation tracks for a variety of issues including:

- Relax and Focus
- Stress Reduction
- Deep relaxation, Meditation
- Higher Self-Esteem, Confidence
- Improve Memory and Recall
- Improve Creativity
- Sleep Now!
- Release Fear of Needles
- Release Fear of Spiders
- Stress Reduction
- Release Social Anxiety
- Migraines
- Stop Smoking

Brain Entrainment can be a powerful tool in helping to overcome a variety of emotional and sensory issues.

For more information on Brain Entrainment, go to swishforfish.com

Chapter 21: Summary

Waves—Not Spoons is not the end of the discussion on energy management. It is simply the next step.

Managing our physical, emotional and social energy is an on-going conversation with new ideas and new strategies.

Multiple Energy Waves

Our goal for this text was to empower the reader with a new perspective on energy management and strategies that went beyond spoon theory.

This was our first edition of Waves—Not Spoons but, hopefully, it will not be our last.

Please feel free to contact us with your questions, comments and ideas.

Sincerely,

Gerald Hughes

Appendix A: Additional Resources

What Personality Type Am I? A Brain-Based Guide to Personality and Relationships is a wealth of information and an essential tool for anyone wishing to further understand the source of behavior in themselves and others.

What Personality Type Am I? includes insights into interpersonal dynamics and why some relationships appear to thrive while others seem to struggle.

Click here for "What Personality Am I?".

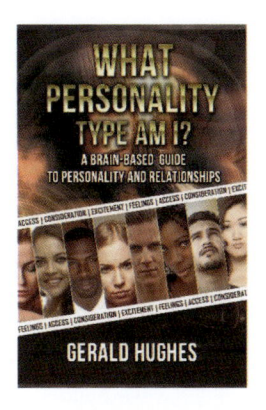

Developed at the Neuro-Linguistic Learning Center in Northern California, Cracking the Dyslexia Code is a clear and simple 10-step program that directly addresses the sensory needs of the child to greatly improve reading, writing, and spelling while building confidence and self-esteem both in and out of the classroom.

Cracking the Dyslexia Code is NOT merely an accommodation or remedial reading program. In addressing the sensory issues of the child, Cracking the Dyslexia Code honors the natural and unique abilities of the child and directly addresses the perceptual issues underlying most reading struggles. **Click here for "Cracking the Dyslexia Code."**

Gifted—Not Broken is an introduction to the sensory profiles underlying Dyslexia, ADHD, and Autism Spectrum Disorders.

This insight into the perception and processing of sensory information opens the door to new understandings and new opportunities to address a number of struggles typically associated with these issues.

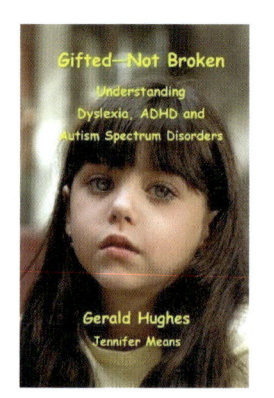

Overcoming Anxiety and Depression is a simple, straightforward Do-it-Yourself Guide to addressing the most common struggles typically associated with Anxiety and Depression.

Overcoming Anxiety and Depression provides clear instructions to real-world strategies, techniques, tips, and tricks to help real people overcome these common struggles.

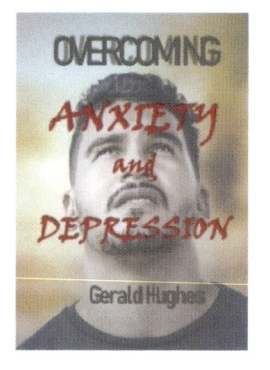

Coming soon from the Neuro-linguistic Learning Center are, "ADHD Survival Guide" and "Autistic Adult Survival Guide".

Additional programs, articles, and videos at **swishforfish.com**

Appendix B: Additional Links

Personality Assessment (online)
https://swishforfish.com/pages/the-face-personality-assessment

Learning/Sensory Assessment (online)
https://swishforfish.com/pages/nlc-sensory-learning-profile

"Relax and Focus" iphone app
https://apps.apple.com/us/app/relax-and-focus/id1460456104?ls=1

"Juggling Made Easy" iphone app
https://apps.apple.com/us/app/juggling-made-easy/id1460449869?ls=1

Memory and Executive Functioning
"A review of the relation between dissociation, memory, executive functioning and social cognition in military members and civilians with neuropsychiatric conditions"

Margaret C. McKinnon, Jenna E.Boyd, Paul A. Frewence, Ulrich F. Laniush, Rakesh Jetly, Donald Richardson, Ruth A. Lanius

https://www.sciencedirect.com/science/article/pii/S0028393216302615

The p Factor: One General Psychopathology Factor in the Structure of Psychiatric Disorders?
"Using the Dunedin Multidisciplinary Health and Development Study, we examined the structure of psychopathology, taking into account dimensionality, persistence, co-occurrence, and sequential comorbidity of mental disorders across 20 years, from adolescence to midlife."

Authors: Avshalom Caspi, Renate M. Houts, Daniel W. Belsky, Sidra J. Goldman-Mellor, HonaLee Harrington, Salomon Israel, Madeline H. Meier, Sandhya Ramrakha, Idan Shalev, Richie Poulton, and Terrie E. Moffitt

https://www.ncbi.nlm.nih.gov/pmc/articles/PMC4209412/

Understanding the stress response: Chronic activation of this survival mechanism impairs health

https://www.health.harvard.edu/staying-healthy/understanding-the-stress-response

Brain Structure and Personality
"Linking how brain structure is related to basic personality traits is a crucial step to improving our understanding of the link between the brain morphology and particular mood, cognitive, or behavioural disorders" - Luca Passamonti

https://www.cam.ac.uk/research/news/personality-traits-linked-to-differences-in-brain-structure

"Neural correlates of emotion–cognition interactions: A review of evidence from brain imaging investigations"
F Dolcos, AD Iordan, S Dolcos - Journal of Cognitive Psychology, 2011 - Taylor & Francis

https://www.tandfonline.com/doi/full/10.1080/20445911.2011.594433

EEG-Imaging Research
"Overlaps and distinctions between attention deficit/hyperactivity disorder and autism spectrum disorder in young adulthood: Systematic review and guiding framework for EEG-imaging research" Alex Lau-Zhu, Anne Fritz, and Gráinne McLoughlin

https://www.ncbi.nlm.nih.gov/pmc/articles/PMC6331660/

References

Amen, Daniel G., M.D. Healing ADHD. The Breakthrough Program That Allows You to See and Heal the Six Types of Attention Deficit Disorder. The Berkley Publishing Group. 2001.

Bandler, Richard. Using Your Brain for A Change. Real People Press, 1985.

Barbe, Walter B., Swassing, Raymond H. Teaching Through Modality Strengths: Concepts and Practices. Zaner-Bloser, Inc.., 1979.

Blackerby, Don A. Ph.D. Rediscover the Joy of Learning. Don Blackerby, Ph.D., 1996.

Bolick, Teresa, Ph.D.. Asperger's Syndrome. Fair Winds Press, 2001.

Davis, Ronald D. The Gift of Dyslexia. Ability Workshop Press, 1994.

Grandin, Temple. Thinking in Pictures and Other Reports From My Life with Autism. Doubleday. 1995.

Hartman, Thomas. Attention Deficit Disorder: A Different Perception. Mythical Intelligence, Inc., 1993.

Hartman, Thomas. The Edison Gene, ADHD and the Gift of the Hunter Child. Park Street Press, 2003.

Valentine, Tom and Carole with Douglas P. Hetrick, D.C.. Applied Kinesiology. Healing Arts Press, 1985.

Waves—Not Spoons

101 Strategies for Managing Our Physical, Emotional, and Social Energy

By Gerald Hughes

Printed in Great Britain
by Amazon